P9-CQC-312

"Two strands of theatre unite brilliantly in Conor McPherson's *The Weir*: the Irish love of fable and the Chekhovian sense of waste. . . . It is a spellbinder that transfixes you. . . . No praise is too high. . . . The Weir is the most exciting evening in theatrical London."

—*London Guardian*

"*The Weir* is the best new play London has seen in years. There is great humor and a deep sense of waste. One element in the story is so tragic that I would normally resist it in a work of fiction as constituting too easy an assault on our feelings. But with McPherson, you never feel that you are being manipulated. There is too much truthfulness and too much concern. His sense of tragedy is matched by a sense of ordinary life going on. He understands both the possibility and the limits of consolation."

—*London Sunday Telegraph*

"*The Weir* is a beautiful play. McPherson manages to ponder loneliness, failure, loss, metaphysical mystery, macho competition, even the identity crisis of rural communities."

—*London Times*

"In its stylistic simplicity and integrity, *The Weir* reveals acute truths about the games we play to protect ourselves and hide the pain of living. It strikes where the best storytellers take aim—deep inside the imagination and the heart."

—*Variety*

"*St. Nicholas* is theatre as storytelling, with stories folded into stories, abundant with humor and a resplendently Irish joy for language."

—*Newsday*

"*This Lime Tree Bower* is an old-fashioned, hardboiled yarn. . . . Another nail biter from this award-winning playwright."

—*London Sunday Times*

"McPherson's one-man play, *Rum and Vodka*, details with appalling attention and mind-numbing fastidiousness every single event that befalls his everyman."

—*London Sunday Tribune*

THE
WEIR

AND

OTHER PLAYS

THE
WEIR

AND
OTHER PLAYS

CONOR
MCPHERSON

THEATRE COMMUNICATIONS GROUP

The Weir and Other Plays is copyright © 1999 by Conor McPherson

The Weir and Other Plays is published by Theatre Communications Group, Inc., 355 Lexington Ave., New York, NY 10017-0217.

Afterword is copyright © 1999 by Conor McPherson
The Weir is copyright © 1997, 1999 by Conor McPherson
St. Nicholas is copyright © 1997, 1999 by Conor McPherson
This Lime Tree Bower is copyright © 1996, 1999 by Conor McPherson
The Good Thief is copyright © 1996, 1999 by Conor McPherson
Rum and Vodka is copyright © 1996, 1999 by Conor McPherson

All rights reserved. Except for brief passages quoted in newspaper, magazine, radio or television reviews, no part of this book may be reproduced in any form or by any means, electronic or mechanical, including photocopying or recording, or by an information storage and retrieval system, without permission in writing from the publisher.

Professionals and amateurs are hereby warned that this material being fully protected under the Copyright Laws of the United States of America and all other countries of the Berne and Universal Copyright Conventions, is subject to a royalty. All rights including, but not limited to, professional, amateur, recording, motion picture, recitation, lecturing, public reading, radio and television broadcasting, and the rights of translation into foreign languages are expressly reserved. Particular emphasis is placed on the question of readings and all uses of this book by educational institutions, permission for which must be secured from the author's representative: Curtis Brown Ltd., Haymarket House, 28–29 Haymarket, London, England SW1Y 4SP.

The Weir and Other Plays is published in arrangement with
Nick Hern Books Limited, The Glasshouse, 49a Goldhawk Rd.,
Shepherd's Bush, London, England W12 8QP.

This publication is made possible in part with public funds from
the New York State Council on the Arts, a State Agency.

LIBRARY OF CONGRESS CATALOGING-IN-PUBLICATION DATA
McPherson, Conor, 1971-
The weir, and other plays / by Conor McPherson. — 1st ed.
p. cm.
ISBN 1–55936–167–0 (pbk. : alk. paper)
1. Ireland—Drama. I. Title.
PR6063.C73W45   1999
822'.914—dc21   99–18988
CIP

Cover, book design and typography by Lisa Govan
Author photo by Susan Johann
Cover photo by Carter Smith/Katy Barker Agency

First edition, April 1999
Second Printing, August 1999
Third Printing, March 2000

To the Actors

CONTENTS

THE WEIR

For Michael, Clare, Karen and Margaret

And for Rionach

The Weir is an ensemble piece where the actors do talk to each other. It's full of ghost stories. This play was probably inspired by my visits to Leitrim to see my grandad. He lived on his own down a country road in a small house beside the Shannon. I remember him telling me once that it was very important to have the radio on because it gave him the illusion of company. We'd have a drink and sit at the fire. And he'd tell me stories.

And then when you're lying in bed in the pitch black silence of the Irish countryside it's easy for the imagination to run riot. I always felt different there. I can still see him standing on the platform at the station. He always waved for much too long. Much longer than a person who was glad to have their privacy back.

Conor McPherson
JANUARY 1997

The Weir was first performed in London's Royal Court Theatre Upstairs on July 4, 1997. The play then moved to the larger Royal Court Theatre Downstairs on February 18, 1998. The production was designed by Rae Smith, the lighting was by Paule Constable. Ian Rickson directed the following cast:

JACK	Jim Norton
BRENDAN	Brendan Coyle
JIM	Kieran Ahern
FINBAR	Gerard Horan (Upstairs)
	Des McAleer (Downstairs)
VALERIE	Julia Ford

The Royal Court's production of *The Weir* received its American premiere on April 1, 1999 at Broadway's Walter Kerr Theatre, Thomas Viertel, Richard Frankel, Steven Baruch, Marc Routh, Jujamcyn Theaters, Manhattan Theatre Club, Turnstyle/Ambassador Theatre Group, producers. Cast changes were as follows:

FINBAR	Dermot Crowley
VALERIE	Michelle Fairley

CHARACTERS

JACK, fifties

BRENDAN, thirties

JIM, forties

FINBAR, late forties

VALERIE, thirties

PLACE

The play is set in a rural part of Ireland,
Northwest Leitrim or Sligo.
Present day. A small rural bar.

A counter, left, with three bar taps. The spirits are not mounted, simply left on the shelf. There are three stools at the counter.

There is a fireplace, right. There is a stove built into it. Near this is a low table with some small stools and a bigger, more comfortable chair, nearest the fire. There is another small table, front, with a stool or two.

On the wall, back, are some old black-and-white photographs: a ruined abbey; people posing near a newly erected ESB weir; a town in a cove with mountains around it.

An old television is mounted up in a corner. There is a small radio on a shelf behind the bar.

A door, right, is the main entrance to the bar. A door, back, leads to the toilets and a yard.

This bar is part of a house, and the house is part of a farm.

The door, right, opens. Jack comes in. He wears a suit, which looks a bit big for him, and a white shirt open at the collar. Over this is a dirty anorak. He takes the anorak off and hangs it up. He wipes his boots aggressively on a mat.

He goes behind the counter. He selects a glass and goes to pour himself a pint of stout. Nothing comes out of the tap. He vainly tries it again and looks underneath the counter. He turns and takes *a bottle from the shelf, awkwardly prizing off the top. He pours it and leaves it on the bar to settle. He turns to the till which he opens with practised, if uncertain, ease. He takes a list of prices from beside the till and holds a pair of spectacles up to his face while he examines it. He puts money in the till and takes his change.*

As he finishes this, the door at back opens. Brendan comes in. He wears a sweater, heavy cord pants and a pair of slip-on shoes. He carries a bucket with peat briquettes. He goes to the fireplace, barely acknowledging Jack, just his voice.

BRENDAN: Jack.

JACK: Brendan. *(Lifting glass)* What's with the Guinness?

BRENDAN *(Putting peat in the stove)*: I don't know. It's the power in the tap. It's a new barrel and everything.

JACK: Is the Harp one okay?

BRENDAN: Yeah.

JACK: Well, would you not switch them around and let a man have a pint of stout, no?

BRENDAN: What about the Harp drinkers?

JACK *(Derision)*: "The Harp drinkers?"

BRENDAN: Your man's coming in to do it in the morning. Have a bottle.

JACK: I'm having a bottle. *(Pause)* I'm not happy about it, now mind, right? But, like.

(They laugh.)

BRENDAN: Go on out of that.

JACK *(Drinks)*: What the hell. Good for the worms.

BRENDAN: I'd say you have a right couple of worms, alright.

(They laugh. Pause. Brendan stands wiping his hands.)

That's some wind, isn't it?

JACK: It is.

BRENDAN: Must have been against you, was it?

(Jack comes out from behind the counter.)

JACK: It was. It was against me till I came around the Knock. It was a bit of shelter then.

(Brendan goes in behind the counter. He tidies up, dries glasses.)

BRENDAN: Yeah it's a funny one. It's coming from the North.

JACK: Mm. Ah, it's mild enough though.

BRENDAN: Ah yeah. It's balmy enough. *(Pause)* It's balmy enough.

JACK: Were you in Carrick today?

BRENDAN: I wasn't, no. I had the sisters over doing their rounds. Checking up on me.

JACK: Checking their investments.

BRENDAN: Oh yeah. 'Course, they don't have a fucking clue what they're looking for, d'you know? They're just vaguely . . . you know.

JACK: Keeping the pressure on you.

BRENDAN: This is it. *(Pause)* At me to sell the top field.

JACK: You don't use it much.

BRENDAN: No. No I don't. Too much trouble driving a herd up. But I know they're looking at it. All they see is new cars for the hubbies, you know?

JACK: Mm. You're not just trying to spite them? Get them vexed, ha?

BRENDAN: Not at all. I'm, just. It's a grand spot up there. Ah, I don't know. Just . . .

(Short pause.)

JACK: They over the whole day?

BRENDAN: They got here about two. They'd gone for lunch in the Arms. Got their story straight. Ah they were gone and all about half four.

JACK: They've no attachment to the place, no?

BRENDAN: No they don't. They look around, and it's . . . "Ah yeah . . ." you know?

(They laugh a little.)

It's gas.

JACK: Mm.

BRENDAN: Were you in Carrick yourself?

JACK: I was. Flew in about eleven, threw on a fast bet. Jimmy was there. We went for a quick one in the Pot.

BRENDAN: How is he? And the ma?

JACK: Ah. Jimmy. Be in tonight. He put me on to a nice one. We got her at eleven to four.

BRENDAN: You're learning to listen, ha?

JACK: Ah. Fuck that sure. I know, but I've been having the worst run of shit you wouldn't believe. I was that desperate, I'd listen to anybody.

BRENDAN: Go on out of that.

JACK: Ah no. No no. Fair dues. I'll say it. He got us a right one. And it's good, you know. Break a streak like that.

BRENDAN: You're a user.

JACK *(Laughs)*: There's worse.

BRENDAN: Yeah. There might be.

JACK: But, ah, he was telling me. Did you know about Maura Nealon's house?

BRENDAN: No.

JACK: Well. Jim says he met Finbar Mack down in the Spar. Finally, either sold or's renting the, the thing, after how many years it's sat there?

BRENDAN: Jays, four or five in anyway.

JACK: Jim says five this month. And Finbar's going bananas with the great fella that he is. Patting himself on the back, goodo, and talking about the new resident. Who, he says, is a fine girl. Single. Down from Dublin and all this. And Finbar's nearly leaving the wife just to have a chance with this one. Only messing, like. But he's bringing her in here tonight, the nearest place. To old . . . Maura's. Bringing her in for a drink. Introduce her to the natives.

BRENDAN: The dirty bastard. I don't want him using in here for that sort of carry on. A married man like him.

JACK: Ah, he's only old shit. He wouldn't have the nerve. Sure, how far'd he get anyway? The fucking head on him. He's only having a little thrill. Bringing her around. And I'll tell you what it is as well. He's coming in here with her. And he's the one. He's the one that's "with" her, in whatever fucking . . . sense we're talking about. He's bringing her in. And there's you and me, and the Jimmy fella, the muggins's, the single fellas. And he's the married fella. And he's going, "Look at this! There's obviously something the fuck wrong with yous. Yous are single and you couldn't get a woman near this place. And look at me. I'm hitched. I'm over and done with, and I'm having to beat them off."

BRENDAN: Yeah. That's the way cunts always go about their business. It's intrusive, it's bad manners, it's . . .

JACK: Ah, it's a juvenile carry on. You know?

BRENDAN: Mm.

JACK: Let her come in herself.

BRENDAN: Yeah. That'd be better. That'd make more sense, for fuck's sake.

JACK: Leave her be. Don't know if I'll stay actually.

BRENDAN: Mm.

(Pause. Jack drains his glass and puts it on the bar.)

JACK: Go on.

(Brendan takes the glass and pours a fresh bottle.)

Don't want to leave Jimmy in the lurch. You know? Trying to hold his own in the Finbar Mack world of big business.

(They laugh a little.)

BRENDAN: Fucking . . . Jimmy talking all that crack with
   Finbar.
JACK: That's the thing though. The Jimmy fella's got more
   going on up here (*Head*) than popular opinion would
   give him credit for.
BRENDAN: Sure, don't we know too well for God's sake?
JACK: I know.
BRENDAN: We know only too well.

(*Jack counts change out on the bar.*)

JACK: Would you give us ten Silk Cut please, Brendan?
BRENDAN: Red?
JACK: Please.

(*Brendan puts the cigarettes on the bar.*)

Good man.

(*Pause. Jack doesn't touch them yet. Brendan counts the money off
the bar. Jack pauses before drinking.*)

Are we right?
BRENDAN: Close enough. Cheers.
JACK: Good luck.

(*Jack takes a long drink. Pause.*)

I know I do be at you. I'll keep at you though.
BRENDAN: About what?
JACK: Don't be messing. Come on.
BRENDAN: Ah.
JACK: A youngfella like you. And this place a right going
   concern.
BRENDAN: Ah. The odd time. You know, the odd time I'd
   think about it.
JACK: You should though.

BRENDAN: Well then, so should you.

JACK: Would you go on? An auldfella like me!

BRENDAN: Would you listen to him?

JACK: Sure what would I want giving up my freedom?

BRENDAN: Well then me as well!

(Pause.)

JACK: Tch. Maybe. Maybe there's something to be said for the old independence.

BRENDAN: Ah there is.

(Pause.)

JACK: A lot to be said for it.

BRENDAN: Mm. *(Pause)* Mm.

JACK: Cheers.

BRENDAN: Good luck.

(Jack takes a long drink. The main door opens and Jim enters. He takes off an anorak to reveal a festive-looking cardigan. Jack pretends not to notice him.)

JACK *(Winks)*: Oh yes, Brendan, the luck is changing. I got me and the Jimmy fella on to a nice one today. That fella'd want to listen to me a bit more often, I tell you.

JIM: I'm going to have to start charging you for tips, am I?

JACK: Ah James! What'll you have?

JIM: Teach you some manners. Teach him some manners Brendan, ha? Small one please, Jack.

BRENDAN: Small one.

JACK: Sure it'd take more than money to put manners on me, ha Brendan?

BRENDAN: It'd take a bomb under you.

JACK: Now you said it. Bomb is right. That wind still up, Jim?

JIM: Oh it is, yeah. Warm enough though.

JACK: We were just saying.

BRENDAN: For a Northerly.
JIM: Oh that's from the West now.
BRENDAN: Is it?
JIM: Oh yeah that's a Westerly.
JACK: Must've shifted.
JIM: Mm.

(*Pause. Jim comes to the bar.*)

JIM: Thanking you.
JACK: Good luck.
JIM: Good luck.
BRENDAN: Good luck.

(*Jack counts change out on the bar.*)

JACK: Are we right?

(*Brendan counts and pushes a coin back towards Jack.*)

BRENDAN (*Gathering coins*): Now we are. Sure it's hard enough
    to come by without giving it away.
JACK: This is it. Oh (*To Jim*) Are you doing anything
    tomorrow?
JIM: What time?
JACK: I have to get out to Conor Boland. His tractor's packed
    up. And I have Father Donal's jalopy in since Tuesday.
    Said I'd change the oil. Haven't done it yet. Would you
    ever come in and do it so I can get over to Boland's?
JIM: It'd have to be early. I'm dropping the mother out to
    Sligo.
JACK: Well, whatever. Is that alright?
JIM: Ah, it should be, yeah. Pint?
JACK: Not for the moment. You go on.
JIM: Pint please Brendan. You on the bottles?

(*Brendan takes a glass and pours Jim a pint of lager from the
good tap.*)

JACK: Ah. Medicinal.

JIM: Ha?

BRENDAN: Ah the tap's fucked.

JIM: I was wondering, Jaysus what's your man fucking doing now, you know?

BRENDAN: Yeah. He'd be the fella'd have a figary and be only drinking bottles from now on. He would. *(To Jack)* You would. Be you to a fucking tee.

(Jack sits as though he has to bear the world with great patience. They laugh. Pause. Jack shakes his head.)

JACK: How's the mammy today?

JIM: Ah, you know?

JACK: Tch. I have to get down and see her. I keep saying it.

JIM *(Tone of "No rush. No pressure")*: Well whenever, whenever you want.

BRENDAN: Do you think you'll do anything?

JIM: About?

BRENDAN: About up there on your own and all that?

JIM: Ah. Sure where would I go? And I was talking to Finbar Mack. Be lucky to get twenty thousand for the place. Sure where would you be going with that? *(Short pause)* You know?

JACK: With the acre?

JIM: Ah yeah, the whole . . . the whole thing.

JACK: Ah you're grand with the few little jobs around here.

JIM: Ah.

JACK: You'll be cozy enough.

(Pause.)

BRENDAN: Jack was telling me about Finbar. And the new eh . . .

JIM: Mmm, yeah. I was telling him earlier.

JACK: I was telling him.

JIM: I've seen her since.

BRENDAN: Oh yeah?

JIM: Yeah, they were in Finbar's car going up the Head.

(Jack and Brendan exchange a look.)

BRENDAN: Fucking hell.

JACK: Like a courting couple or something.

JIM: He's showing her the area.

JACK: Jesus. "The area." He's a terrible fucking thick. What the fuck is he doing? You know?

JIM: Ah. She's . . . This is the only place near to her.

JACK: She can . . . *(Nodding)* find her own way surely, Jim, come on.

BRENDAN: Well it's, you know. If it's courtesy, which is one thing, and a business . . . act or whatever, you know, you have to say, well okay and . . . But if it's all messy, I'm trapped in here behind this fucking thing. And you wish he'd stop acting the mess. I have to respect whatever, they're . . .

JACK: Well this is it, we're here.

JIM: It's probably not really anything.

(Short pause.)

JACK: What age would she be, about, Jim?

JIM: Em. I only saw her for a sec. I'd say, *(Beat)* like they were in the car and all. I'd say about thirties. Very nice looking.

(Pause.)

JACK: Dublin woman.

JIM: Dublin.

(Short pause.)

BRENDAN: She's no one in the area, no?

JIM: No she's . . . coming down, you know?

JACK: Mm. *(Pause)* Yeah.

JIM: Good luck. *(Drinks)*

JACK: Cheers. *(Drinks)*

BRENDAN: Good luck, boys.

JACK: Another week or two now, you'll be seeing the first of the Germans.

BRENDAN: Mm. Stretch in the evening, yeah.

JACK: You still wouldn't think about clearing one of the fields for a few caravans.

BRENDAN: Ah.

JACK: The top field.

BRENDAN: Ah there wouldn't be a lot of shelter up there, Jack. There'd be a wind up there that'd cut you.

JIM: D'you know what you could do? The herd'd be grand up there, and you could, you know, down here.

BRENDAN: Ah. *(Short pause)* They do be around anyway. You know yourself.

JIM: Ah, they do.

JACK: You're not chasing the extra revenue.

BRENDAN: Or the work!

JIM: They do be around right enough.

BRENDAN: I'll leave the campsites to Finbar, ha? He'll sort them out.

JACK: Ah, Finbar's in real need of a few shekels.

(They laugh.)

BRENDAN: Ah he's in dire need of a few bob, the poor fella, that's right, that's right.

JACK: Mm.

(Pause.)

BRENDAN: Yeah. If you had all . . . the families out there. On their holliers. And all the kids and all. You'd feel the evenings turning. When they'd be leaving. And whatever about how quiet it is now. It'd be fucking shocking quiet then. *(Short pause)* You know?

(Pause.)

JACK: Mm.
JIM: D'you want a small one, Jack?
JACK: Go on.
JIM: Two small ones please, Brendan.
BRENDAN: The small fellas.

(Brendan works. Jim counts some change on to the bar.)

JACK: Are you having one yourself tight?
BRENDAN: I'm debating whether to have one.
JACK: Ah, have one and don't be acting the mess.
BRENDAN: Go on then.

(Brendan pours himself a glass of whiskey.)

JACK: Good man. *(Counts change on to the bar)* A few shekels, ha? *(They smile)* Mm.

(Jack takes out his cigarettes.)

Jim?
JIM: Oh cheers Jack.

(Jim takes one.)

JACK: Brendan?
BRENDAN: Fags and all, ha?
JACK: Go on. They're good for you.
BRENDAN *(Taking one)*: Go on.

(They light up from a match which Jack strikes. They puff contentedly for a moment.)

JIM *(Lifting glass)*: Keep the chill out.
JACK: This is it. Cheers.
BRENDAN: Cheers men.
JIM: Good luck.

(They drink.)

JACK: Now.
JIM: D'yous hear a car?

(Pause.)

BRENDAN: No.
JIM: That's Finbar's car.

(Pause.)

JIM: He's parked.
JACK: I didn't see the lights.
JIM: He came around the Knock.

(From off they hear Finbar's voice.)

FINBAR *(Off)*: Ah yeah, sure half the townland used to nearly live in here.
JACK: There we are now.

(The door opens and Finbar brings Valerie in.)

FINBAR: That's it now.

(Finbar wears a light cream-colored suit and an open collar. Valerie wears jeans and a sweater. She carries a jacket.)

FINBAR: Men. This is Valerie. She's just moved into Maura Nealon's old house.

JACK: Hello, how are you?

(*Jack shakes her hand.*)

VALERIE: Hello.

FINBAR: This is Jack Mullen. He has a little garage up around the Knock.

(*Jack nods politely.*)

JACK: Now.

FINBAR: This is Jim Curran. Does a bit of work with Jack.

(*Valerie shakes hands with Jim.*)

VALERIE: Pleased to meet you.

JIM: Pleased to meet you.

FINBAR: And this Brendan. Brendan Byrne.

VALERIE: Hello.

(*They shake hands.*)

BRENDAN: How are you?

FINBAR: This is his bar. And all the land I showed you. All back down the hill. That's all his farm.

VALERIE: Oh right. It's all lovely here.

BRENDAN: Oh yeah. It's a grand spot all along . . . for going for a walk or that, all down the cliffs.

FINBAR: Oh it's lovely all around here. What'll you have?

BRENDAN: Oh, I'll get this, Finbar. No. What, what do you want?

FINBAR: Oh now, ha ha. Eh, I'll have a pint then, what, says you, if it's going, ha? Eh Harp please Brendan.

(*Jack looks at Finbar. Finbar nods at him.*)

Jack.

JACK: Finbar.

BRENDAN: What would you like, Valerie?

VALERIE: Em. Could I have . . . Do you have . . . em, a glass of white wine?

(Pause.)

BRENDAN *(Going):* Yeah. I'm just going to run in the house.

VALERIE: Oh no. Don't. Don't put yourself to any trouble.

BRENDAN: No. No it's no trouble. I have a bottle.

(Brendan goes.)

FINBAR: He probably has a bottle of the old vino, from feckin . . . Christmas, ha?

JACK: It's not too often the . . . the . . . wine does be flowing in here.

VALERIE: I'm all embarrassed now.

FINBAR: Don't be silly. Sit up there now, and don't mind us. Don't mind these country fellas.

JACK: Jays. You're not long out of it yourself, says the man, ha?

FINBAR *(Winks):* They're only jealous Valerie because I went the town to seek my fortune. And they all stayed out here on the bog picking their holes.

JACK: Janey, now, ha? You didn't have very far to seek. Just a quick look in Big Finbar's will, I think is more like it.

FINBAR: Big Finbar's will! That's shrewd investment, boy. That's an eye for the gap.

JACK: Yeah, he probably fleeced you on Maura Nealon's house, did he?

VALERIE: I have to say I don't think so.

FINBAR: Good girl.

VALERIE: But it's very reasonable all around here, isn't it?

FINBAR: Oh it is, yeah. You know . . .

(Short pause.)

JACK: Is there much doing up on it?

FINBAR: Ah, hardly any.

VALERIE (*Checking with Finbar*): There's one or two floor-boards. Bit of paint.

JACK (*Indicating Jim*): Well, there's your man. If you're looking for a good pair of hands.

VALERIE: Is that right?

JIM: I'll have a look for you, if you like. I know that house.

FINBAR: Don't be charging her through the nose now.

JIM: Ah ha, now.

(*Brendan returns with a bottle of wine.*)

FINBAR: You'd want to be giving her a neighborly . . . rate, now, is the thing, ha?

JIM: Oh yeah.

JACK: Would you listen to him? "Neighborly rates . . ." Wasn't by giving neighborly rates you bought half the fucking town.

FINBAR: Half the town! (*To Valerie, winking*) I bought the whole town. Eye for the gap, you see.

JACK: Eye for your gap is right.

FINBAR (*To Brendan*): How long has that been in there? Lying in some drawer . . .

BRENDAN (*Corkscrewing the bottle*): Ah, it was a . . . present or some . . . (*Looks at label*) 1990. Now. Vintage, ha?

(*They laugh.*)

I hope it's alright now.

VALERIE: It's grand. I won't know the difference.

(*They watch Brendan open the bottle. He pours a tumbler full, then holds it up to the light and sniffs it.*)

BRENDAN: I think it's alright.

FINBAR: Ah would you give the woman the feckin' thing. The tongue's hanging out of her.

(They watch as Valerie takes the glass.)

VALERIE: Thanks Brendan.

(They watch her drink.)

VALERIE: That's gorgeous. I'm not joking now. That's lovely.
FINBAR: Good.
BRENDAN: I'm putting it in the fridge for you, Valerie.
(He does)

(Pause. Finbar nods at Valerie, a reassuring "Hello.")

FINBAR *(To Jack and Jim)*: How d'yous do today, boys?
JACK: Are you codding me? With this fella? Eleven to four we got her at. Came down to six to four.
FINBAR: Sheer Delight, was it?
JACK: Yeah. Kenny down in the shop, the knacker. Adjusting everything how this fella's betting.
BRENDAN: Look who's talking.
JACK: Yeah right.
JIM: He hardly ever listens to me.
JACK: Well. Now . . .
FINBAR: He's too proud, Jimmy. Too proud to admit when he needs a tip off you.
JACK *(Emphatically)*: I . . . have . . . my policy on this. And I have my principle. I am the first one to say it about this fella. See, usually, Valerie, usually, not all the time, Jim's not too far off the mark.
FINBAR: "Too far off the mark"! *(To Valerie)* He's bang on the nail.

(Brendan places a pint on the bar.)

Thanks Brendan. *(He puts his hand in his pocket)*
JACK: Not every time. Jim.

(Brendan waves Finbar away.)

FINBAR: Thanks, thanks a million. *(To Valerie)* He is.
JACK: Bang on the nail is one thing, from judgment . . .
and . . . But, and Jimmy knows I don't mean anything
by this, and I know because we've spoken about this
before. He has a scientific approach. He studies the
form. And, no offense, he has a bit of time to be
doing that. He studies it Valerie, and fair play to him,
right? Do you bet on horses?
VALERIE: No.
FINBAR: Good girl.
JACK: Well he, how much, Jim, would you make in a
month? On the horses.
JIM: Ah it evens out Jack. Like I'm not eh . . . I don't . . .
JACK: How much was it you got that time? When
Cheltenham was on that time.
JIM: Two hundred and twenty.
JACK: Two hundred and twenty pounds, Valerie, in like
three days, now. Right?
JIM: Yeah but . . .
JACK: Yeah, I know, that'd be a bigger win. But he was plan-
ning for Cheltenham for weeks, Valerie, and . . . tinker-
ing with his figures and his . . . you know. He'd be in
here with the paper up on the counter there. Brendan?
Before Cheltenham?
BRENDAN: Yeah.
JACK: Right? Now, but I'm more: Ah, sure, I'll have an old
bet, like. Do you know that way? And that's what I do,
and to tell you the truth I don't be too bothered. It's a
bit of fun and that's what it should be. And so . . . I'm
not going to listen to, Do this and do that, and you'll
be right. Just to get a few bob. There's no fun in that
and the principle of it, you know?

FINBAR: Ah, the principle of the thing is to win a few quid and don't be giving out.

JACK: Who's giving out? I'm not giving out. All I'm saying is that the way I go at it, the principle's not the science. It's the luck, it's the something that's not the facts and figures of it.

FINBAR: Jaysus. And do you and Kenny get down on your knees and lash a few quick Hail Marys out before he stamps your docket or something?

JACK: Ah it's not like that. I'm not talking about that. For fuck's sake.

FINBAR: Anyway, what the hell are you talking about? You took Jimmy's tip today, and you won so what the hell are you talking about? *(To others)* Ha?

JACK: Ah yeah but . . . now listen because . . .

(The others are laughing, going "Ah" as though Finbar has caught Jack out.)

I'll tell yous. If you won't listen . . . Right? I don't have a system. And I do. I do lose a few bob every now and then. Right? So I take a little tip from Jim. And then that'll finance having a couple of bets over the next few weeks.

(They laugh.)

And I've been known to have one or two wins myself, as well yous know and don't forget. I have one or two.

BRENDAN: You do not. Go on out of that you chancer.

JACK: I do.

FINBAR: I'd say the last win you had was fucking Red Rum or someone.

JACK *(Aside to Valerie)*: We do be only messing like this.

FINBAR: What would anyone like? Jim?

JIM: Eh, small one then, thanks, Finbar.

FINBAR: Jack? Small one? Pint? Bottle, is it? You on the bottles?

JACK: No the tap is . . . fucking . . .

FINBAR: Oh. Typical.

JACK: Ah, I'll have a small one, go on.

FINBAR: Good man. Valerie?

VALERIE: Oh no, I'm okay for the moment, thanks.

FINBAR: Are you sure? Top that up?

VALERIE: No I'm fine, honestly.

FINBAR: You're sure now?

VALERIE: No really, I'm fine.

FINBAR (*Hands up*): Fair enough. We won't force you. Give us . . . eh, three small ones, Brendan. Good man. Here, are you having one?

BRENDAN (*Working*): I'm debating whether to have one.

JACK: Ah, he'll have one. Go on Brendan. Who knows when the hell you'll see another drink off the Finbar fella, ha? Come on! Quick! He's all annoyed you're having one.

FINBAR (*To Valerie*): Would you listen to him?

JACK: That fella'd peel a banana in his pocket.

JIM: Is that what it is?

(*They laugh.*)

FINBAR: First time I've been in here for ages, bringing nice company in and everything, getting this. Oh you'd have to watch the Jimmy fella. There's more going on there than he lets on. "Is that what that is?"

(*Brendan places the drinks on the bar.*)

And look at this! Me buying the drinks like a feckin eejit. Ah it's not right. What do you think Valerie?

VALERIE: Oh it's terrible.

FINBAR: Oh, it's desperate. (*He hands Brendan a twenty-pound note*) There you go, Brendan. I wouldn't say you see too many twenties in here. With the boys, wouldn't be too often, I'd say. Cheers boys.

JACK (*To Brendan*): Check that. Cheers.

JIM: Good luck.

BRENDAN: Good luck now.

VALERIE: Cheers.

JACK: How did you put up with that fella showing you around?

VALERIE: Ah, he was a bit quieter today.

JACK: Well. You're seeing the real him now. And I bet you prefer the other one. We've never seen it. The quiet Finbar. This one comes out at night, you see.

VALERIE: Oh, well I was getting the history of the place and everything today.

JACK: "The history of the place." You were probably making it all up on the spot, were you?

FINBAR: Yeah, I was, yeah. That's why all them photographs are fake. I had them done years ago just to fool Valerie, tonight.

VALERIE *(Going to the photographs)*: Oh right. That's all around here, is it?

FINBAR *(Going to the photographs)*: That's the weir. When was that taken, Brendan?

BRENDAN: Eh, that's 1951.

FINBAR: 1951. The weir, the river, the weir, em is to regulate the water for generating power for the area and for Carrick as well. *(To Brendan)* That's your dad there.

BRENDAN: Yeah. I think your dad's in it too.

FINBAR: Oh he is! Valerie, look at this. That's Big Finbar now. And that's Brendan's father, Paddy Byrne. This was when the ESB opened it. Big thing around here, Brendan.

BRENDAN: Oh yeah.

VALERIE *(To Finbar)*: You look like your father. *(To Brendan)* You don't.

FINBAR: He's like his mother. He's like the Mangans. Now . . . Who would you say that is there. In the shorts.

VALERIE: Is it you?

FINBAR: Would you go on? The big fucking head on that yoke! Excuse the language. That's Jack.

VALERIE: Oh my God! How old were you there, Jack?

JACK: Em. Oh I was about seven.

VALERIE: I wouldn't have said that was you.

FINBAR: You must be joking, you'd spot that big mutton head anywhere. The photographer nearly had to ask him to go home, there wasn't going to be room in the picture. Isn't that right Jack?

JACK: That's right, and your dad nearly climbing into the camera there.

FINBAR: He was a pillar of the community, Valerie. No one had anything against him. Except headers like your man there. (*Indicating Jack*)

JACK: That's right, Finbar. And I'm just going in here to do something up against the pillar of the community now.

(*Jack goes out door at back.*)

FINBAR: Jays, he's a desperate fella, that one.

VALERIE: Where was this taken?

BRENDAN: That's the view of Carrick from our top field up there.

VALERIE: It's an amazing view.

FINBAR: Oh I'd say that's probably one of the best views all around here, wouldn't it be?

BRENDAN: Oh yeah I'd say so.

JIM: Oh yeah, it would be, yeah.

FINBAR: You get all the Germans trekking up here in the summer, Valerie. Up from the campsite.

VALERIE: Right.

FINBAR: They do come up. This'd be the scenic part of all around here, you know? Em. There's what's? There was stories all, the fairies be up there in that field. Isn't there a fort up there?

BRENDAN: There's a kind of a one.

VALERIE: A fairy fort?

FINBAR: The Germans do love all this.

BRENDAN: Well there's a . . . ring of trees, you know.

FINBAR: What's the story about the fairy road that . . . Who used to tell it?

BRENDAN: Ah, Jack'd tell you all them stories.

FINBAR: There's all this around here, Valerie, the area's steeped in old folklore, and that, you know.

BRENDAN: Jack'd know . . . the what the, you'd know a few, Jim.

JIM: Ah Jack'd tell you better than me.

FINBAR *(At photograph)*: That's the abbey now.

VALERIE: Oh yeah.

FINBAR: You can see more of it there now. What was there, Brendan? When was that?

BRENDAN: Oh, back in oh, fifteen something, there was a synod of bishops all came and met there for . . . like . . . eh.

JIM: This townland used to be quite important back a few hundred years ago, Valerie. This was like the capital of the, the county, it would have been.

VALERIE: Right.

(Jack comes back in.)

FINBAR: Oh it's a very interesting place all, eh, Jack we were just saying about the, what was the story with the fairy road?

JACK: The fairy road? I go into the toilet for two minutes. I can't leave yous alone for two minutes . . .

(They laugh.)

FINBAR: Ah I was telling Valerie about the fort and every-thing. What was the story with the fairy road? Where was it?

(Short pause.)

JACK: Are you really interested? All the babies.

FINBAR: Ah it's a bit of fun. Tell her. Where was it?

JACK (*To Finbar*): You're going to regret me saying this now, 'cause you know whose house it was?

FINBAR: Whose?

JACK: It was Maura Nealon's house.

FINBAR (*Self-chastising, remembering*): Oh . . . Jesus.

(*They laugh.*)

JACK: You see? That's as much cop as you have now.

FINBAR: I fucking forgot it was Maura.

JACK: These are only old stories, Valerie.

VALERIE: No. I'd like to hear it.

JACK: It's only an old cod, like.

FINBAR: You're not going to be scaring the woman.

JACK: Ah it's not scary.

VALERIE: I'm interested in it.

FINBAR: You hear all old shit around here, it doesn't mean anything.

BRENDAN: This is a good little story.

JACK: It's only short. It's just. Maura . . . Nealon used to come in here in the evening, sit over there at the fire. How old was she, Jim? When she died?

JIM: Oh Jays, she would have been nearly ninety.

JACK: But she was a grand, you know, spritely kind of a woman till the end. And had all her . . . She was on the ball, like, you know? And she swore that this happened. When she was only a girl. She lived in that house all her life. And she had older brothers and sisters. She was the youngest. And her mother, eh . . .

JIM: Bridie.

JACK: Bridie. She was a well-known woman in the area. A widow woman. She was a bit of a character. Bit of a practical joker and that, you know? And Maura would say that when she was young, she was, Bridie was, always doing things on the older kids, hiding their . . . clothes and all this, you know? And she'd tell them old fibs about what a certain, prospective boyfriend or girl-friend had said about them out on the road and this about coming courting or that. And she was always shouting from upstairs or this, There's someone at the door. She was always saying, There's someone at the back door or there's someone coming up the path. You know. This. And there'd never be, anyone there. And people got used to her. That she liked her joke.

And Maura used to say that one Saturday evening back in about 1910 or 1911, the older ones were getting ready to go out for a dance or whatever was happening. And the mother, Bridie, came down the stairs and said, "Did no one get the door?"

And they were all, "Oh here we go," you know? But—Bridie came down and *opened* the door, and there was nobody there. And she didn't say anything, And she wasn't making a big thing out of it, you know? And Maura said, she was only young, but she knew there was something wrong. She wasn't cracking the jokes. And later on, when the others were all out, it was just her and her mother sitting at the fire. And her mother was very quiet. Normally she'd send Maura up to bed, early enough, like. But Maura said she remembered this night because Bridie didn't send her up. She wanted someone with her, you see. And in those days, Valerie, as you know, there was no electricity out here.

And there's no dark like a winter night in the country. And there was a wind like this one tonight, howling and whistling in off the sea. You hear it under the door and it's like someone singing. Singing in under the door at you. It was this type of night now. Am I setting the scene for you?

(*They laugh.*)

Finbar's looking a bit edgy. You want to finish that small one, I think.

FINBAR: Don't mind my small one. You're making very
heavy weather of this yarn, Jack.

JACK: Ah now, you have to enjoy it. You have to relish the
details of something like this, ha?

(They laugh.)

So there they were, sitting there, and Bridie was staring
into the fire, a bit quiet. And smiling now and again at
Maura. But Maura said she could see a bit of wet in
her eyes. And then there was a soft knocking at the
door. Someone. At the front door. And Bridie never
moved. And Maura said, "Will I get the door,
Mammy?" And Bridie said, "No, sure, it's only someone playing a joke on us, don't mind them." So they
sat there, and there was no more knocking for a while.
And, em, in those days, there was no kitchen. Where
the extension is, Valerie, that was the back door and
only a little latch on it, you know? And that's where
the next knocking was. Very soft, Maura said, and very
low down the door. Not like where you'd expect a
grown man or a woman to be knocking, up here, you
know? And again Bridie was saying, ah, it's only someone having a joke, they'll go away. And then it was at
the window. Maura couldn't see anything out in the
night, and her mother wouldn't let her go over. And
then it stopped. But when it was late and the fire went
down, Bridie wouldn't get up to get more turf for the
fire. Because it was out in the shed. So they just sat
there until the others came back, well after midnight.

VALERIE: What was it?

JACK: Well Maura said her mother never told the others,
and one day when it was only the two of them there,
a priest came and blessed the doors and the windows.
And there was no more knocking then. And it was
only years later that Maura heard from one of the
older people in the area that the house had been built

on what they call a fairy road. Like it wasn't a road,
but it was a . . .

JIM: It was like a row of things.

JACK: Yeah, like a . . . From the fort up in Brendan's top field
there, then the old well, and the abbey further down,
and into the cove where the little pebbly beach is, there.
And the . . . legend would be that the fairies would come
down that way to bathe, you see. And Maura Nealon's
house was built on what you'd call . . . that . . . road.

VALERIE: And they wanted to come through.

JACK: Well that'd be the idea. But Maura never heard the
knocking again except on one time in the fifties when
the weir was going up. There was a bit of knocking
then she said. And fierce load of dead birds all in the
hedge and all this, but that was it. That's the story.

FINBAR: You're not bothered by that, are you Valerie? 'Cause
it's only old cod, you know? You hear all these around,
up and down the country.

VALERIE: Well. I think there's probably something in them.
No, I do.

JACK: Ah, there . . . might be alright. But . . . it doesn't hurt.
A bit of an old story, like. But I'll tell you what, it'd
give you a thirst, like. You know? What'll yous have?

(*They laugh.*)

Valerie, top that up.

VALERIE: Em . . .

JACK: Go on.

FINBAR: Ah she will. Brendan.

(*Brendan puts a clean tumbler on the bar.*)

VALERIE: This glass is fine.

FINBAR: Oh, country ways! Good girl.

(*They laugh. Brendan pours wine.*)

JACK: Finbar. Pint?

FINBAR: Ah. Pint. Why not, says you, ha?

JACK: Jim?

JIM: Ah.

JACK: Two pints and one of these please, Brendan.

BRENDAN: Two pints.

(Pause. Brendan works.)

FINBAR: Yep. Oh yeah.

JACK: Are you debating to have one yourself?

BRENDAN: I'm debating.

FINBAR: Who's winning?

BRENDAN: Ah, it's a draw. I'm going to have a glass.

FINBAR: Good man. Have two, ha?

(They laugh. Jack produces cigarettes.)

JACK: Valerie?

VALERIE: Eh, I will, thanks.

FINBAR *(Pleasantly surprised)*: Oh! Good girl.

JACK: Finbar?

FINBAR: No I won't, thanks Jack. Haven't had one of them
fellas now, eighteen years this November.

JACK: Eighteen years, ha?

(Jack offers the pack to Brendan and Jim who both take one.)

FINBAR: Eighteen years. Not since I made the move. *(To
Valerie)* Down to . . . Carrick.

JACK: I remember this. *(Lighting cigarettes)* Jays, you don't look
any better for it, ha?

(They laugh.)

FINBAR: Oh yeah? We'll see who'd look the better after a
round or two of the fisty footwork ha? And you with
the lungs hanging out your back.

JACK: Jaysus. An auldfella like me. Ten or more years between us and you wanting to give me a few digs. Business . . . killer instinct, is it?

FINBAR *(Winks at Valerie)*: That's an eye for the gap. Exploit the weakness.

JACK: The weakness, yeah? Because talking of the fairy road. Didn't you have a little run in with the fairies or who was it, that time before you went?

FINBAR: Ah, now . . . Jaysus.

JACK: Because you were very brave that time, weren't you?

FINBAR: Ah Jack, for fuck's sake.

JACK: Ah come on now. You were great that time.

FINBAR: You're a bollocks.

JACK: Well, you. You know, talking of the fairies, now you know?

FINBAR: It wasn't the fairies. It was the . . . Walsh young one having us all on. It was only a cod, sure.

JIM: She's in America now. Niamh Walsh.

BRENDAN: It was Niamh that time, yeah?

FINBAR: Ah she was a header. Looking for attention.

VALERIE: What happened?

JACK: This was the brave fella.

FINBAR: Ah stop. It was nothing.

JACK: This was a family lived up beside Big Finbar's place. The Walshes.

FINBAR: Ah they were only blow-ins, he was a guard.

VALERIE: Blow-ins like me?

FINBAR: Ah no. You know what I mean.

JACK: Jays, you'll be losing business with them kind of remarks, ha? Valerie will agree with me there now.

(They laugh.)

FINBAR: Ah she knows what I mean. Valerie's very welcome. She knows that, don't you?

JACK: Ah leave her alone, you're embarrassing everybody now. Jaysus.

(They laugh.)

Tell her the story.

FINBAR: Ah Janey. Sure you have her in a haunted house already! She won't be able to sleep.

VALERIE: No. I'd like to hear it.

FINBAR: It's not even a real one.

JACK: Ah, she wants to hear one, don't be moaning and tell her, come on.

FINBAR: Tch. Just a crowd of headbangers is all it was. There was a house out near where we were on the other side of the Knock there. It would have been the nearest place to us, Valerie, about a quarter mile down the road. And the old lad Finnerty, lived on his own down there, and his family got him into a nursing home out by them down in Westport. And the people who moved in were the Walshes, and your man was a sergeant in the guards, stationed in Carrick. And, like he was fifty-odd and still only a sergeant, so, like, he was no Sherlock Holmes. You know?

(They laugh.)

He wasn't "Walsh of the Yard" or anything like that. And they moved in. He had three daughters who were teenagers, and a youngfella who was married back near Longford there. So the . . . daughters were with him and the missus. And I knew them a little bit because that was the year Big Finbar died, God rest him, and they arrived about the time of the funeral so . . . you know, I met them, then. And I was living on my own because me and Big Finbar were the only two in it at that time. So I was the bachelor boy, and a gaggle of young ones after moving in next door. Yo ho! You know?

(They laugh.)

And around that time I would have been wondering what to do, Valerie, do you know? Whether to sell it on or farm it or, you know. I was twenty-two, twenty-three, you know? And it was, it would have been around eleven or twelve o' clock this night and there was a knock at the door and it was Mrs. Walsh. And she was all upset and asking me if I could come in, she didn't know what to do. The husband was at work, out on a call, and she didn't know anyone in the area, and there was a bit of trouble. So, "What kind of trouble?" I says. And she says she was after getting a phone call from the young one, Niamh, and she was after doing the Luigi board, or what do you call it?

VALERIE: Ouija board.

FINBAR: Ouija board.

JACK: "Luigi board!" She was down there in the chipper in Carrick, was she, Finbar?

FINBAR: Ah fuck off. I meant the Ouija board. You know what I meant. She was after being down in . . .

JACK: "The Luigi board."

FINBAR: She was after, come on now, she was after being down in a friend of hers' house or this. And they were after doing the . . . Ouija board. And she phoned her mother to come and collect her. They said they were after getting a spirit or this, you know, and she was scared, saying it was after her.

And I obviously just thought, this was a load of bollocks, you know? If you'll . . . excuse the language, Valerie. But here was the mother saying she'd gone and picked her up. I mean, like, sorry, but I thought it was all a bit mad. But on the way back they'd seen something, like the mother had seen it as well. Like a dog on the road, running with the car and running after it. Like there's dogs all around here, Valerie, you know? The farmers have them. There was a big dog up there, Jack, that Willie McDermott had that time.

JACK: Oh Jaysus, yeah, it was like a, if you saw it from the distance, you'd think it was a little horse. It was huge.

JIM: Saxon.

FINBAR: That was it. Saxon.

JIM: It was an Irish Wolfhound. He got it off a fella in the North.

FINBAR: Yeah it was huge. You'd be used to seeing dogs all around the place. All kinds, but they'd be tame, like. Their bark'd be worse than their bite. So I wasn't too . . . taken with this story. But she wanted me to come down to the house, because when they'd got back to the house, the young one, Niamh, was going hysterical saying there was something on the stairs. Like, no one else could see it. But she could. And it was a, a woman, looking at her. And Mrs. Walsh didn't know what to do. They couldn't contact the hubbie, and would I come down? I mean, what made her think there was anything I could do, I don't know. But she was panicking, you know . . . So I got in the car and we went down. And Jesus, now, I've never seen the like of it. The young one was in . . . bits. They had a blanket around her and she was as white, now as . . . (Points to Jack's shirt) as white as that. Well whiter, because that's probably filthy.

JACK: Ha ha.

FINBAR: But I'm not messing. And she wouldn't come out of the living room. Because she said there was a woman on the stairs. And I said, what's the woman doing? And she said, "She's just looking at me." She was terrified. Now I didn't know whether she was after taking drugs or drink or what she was after doing. So I says to phone for Dr. Joe in Carrick. This is Joe Dillon, Valerie, you'd see him in the town, he still has his surgery there beside the Spar. Very nice fella. And I got through to him, and he was on his way, and the Niamh one was shouting at me to close the living room door. Because I was out in the hall where the

phone was, and she could see the woman looking at
her over the bannister. Like she was that bad, now. So
Mrs. Walsh phoned Father Donal, got him out of bed.
And fair dues, like, he came down and sort of blessed
the place a little bit. Like he'd be more Vatican Two.
There wouldn't be much of all the demons or that
kind of carryon with him.

JACK: Jaysus, sure, he'd collapse. He's like that, *(Holds up little
finger)* Him and a demon . . .

(They laugh.)

FINBAR: But Dr. Joe gave her a sedative and off she went
then, you know. And we all had a little drink, and
poor Mrs. Walsh was understandably, very, you know,
shaken and everything. But Father Donal told her not
to mind the Ouija, and it was only an old cod. And it
was Niamh's imagination and all this. And then the
phone rang, right? And it was the youngfella, the
brother who was married back in Longford. And he
was all, that his baby was crying and he had it out of
the cot and he was standing at the window and there
was all this commotion next door. Cars in the drive
and all. That an aul one who lived next door who used
to mind Niamh and the other sisters when they were
young and all this, who was bedridden had been found
dead at the bottom of the stairs. She fallen down, and
they found her. And alright, whatever, coincidence.
But . . . eh, that night, at home, I was sitting at the fire
having a last fag before the sack, and, Jack'd know the
house, the stairs come down into the, the main room.
And I had my back to it. To the stairs. And it's stupid
now, but at the time I couldn't turn around. I couldn't
get up to go to bed. Because I thought there was something on the stairs. *(Low laugh)*
And I just sat there, looking at an empty fireplace.
And I sat there until it got bright. I was like a boy, you

know? I wouldn't move in case something saw me. You know that way. I wouldn't even light another fag. Like I was dying for one, and I wouldn't . . . mad. But when it was bright then, I was grand, you know? Obviously there was nothing there and everything, but that was the last fag I ever had. *(Short pause)* They moved away though, then, after that, the Walshes. *(Pause)* Yep.

VALERIE: And that was when you moved. Down to Carrick.

FINBAR: Yeah *(Nods slowly)* Maybe that . . . had something to do with it. I don't know.

VALERIE: Mm.

JACK: Moving down into the lights, yeah?

FINBAR: Mmm. Might be. Might be, alright. Didn't want the loneliness maybe, you know? *(Pause)* Yous all think I'm a loolah now.

(They laugh.)

Ha? I'm the header says you, ha? I'm going to powder my nose I think.

(Finbar goes out door, back.)

JACK *(Calling after him)*: Sure, we knew you were a head-banger. Knew that all along.

(They laugh. Pause.)

Yeah.

VALERIE: I'd imagine though, it can get very quiet.

JACK: Oh it can, yeah. Ah, you get used to it. Brendan.

BRENDAN: Ah yeah you don't think about it.

JACK: Me and Brendan are the fellas on our own. Jim has the mammy to look after, but we're, you know, you can come in here in the evenings. During the day you'd be working. You know, there's company all around. Bit of a community all spread around the place, like.

JIM: You can put the radio on.

(Pause.)

JACK: Have you got any plans or that, for . . . here?
VALERIE: Not really, I'm just going to try and have some . . .
JACK: Peace and quiet.
VALERIE: Mm.
JACK: Jaysus, you're in the right place, so, ha?

(They laugh.)

You're going to have a peace and quiet . . . over . . . load. Oh yeah.
BRENDAN: Sure, you can always stick the head in here. Or Jack, or me or whatever, be able to sort you out for anything.
VALERIE: Thanks. I should be okay.
JACK: You're only ten minutes up the road. And Jaysus, by the looks of things you'll have a job keeping Finbar away, ha?
VALERIE: Ah he's a dote.
JACK: Jays, I've never heard him called that before, ha? Lots of other things, never that though.

(Finbar comes back.)

FINBAR: What have you fecking heard? What are you talking about this time, Mullen, ha? About how twenty Germans were poisoned by the drink in here, last summer. *(Winks at Brendan)* Ha?
JACK: No, I'd say the Arms is the place where that kind of carry-on happens. You'd get a pint in there, now, I believe, that'd put you on your back for a fortnight.
FINBAR: Don't mind them, Valerie, they're only jealous.
VALERIE: That's probably what it is, alright.
FINBAR: You see now? At least there's one person on my side.

JACK: Yeah, right. She's only sticking up for you to make sure she gets a lift after you scaring the living daylights out of her with your insistence on spooky stories.

FINBAR: Go on. It's only headers like me get a fright like that, ha? Fecking loolahs.

(They laugh. Jim counts some money.)

JIM: Does eh . . . Is anybody?

JACK: Ah no, Jim, I'm grand, you look after yourself.

JIM: Are you sure? Valerie?

VALERIE: I'll get you one.

FINBAR: Ah no Valerie, you're . . .

JACK: No, you're alright.

FINBAR: You're the guest. You're the guest.

JIM: Will you have a small one, Finbar?

FINBAR: Eh no, Jim. Thanks very much, I'm fine for the moment, finish this pint.

BRENDAN: Small one Jim? *(Pouring whiskey)*

JIM: Thanks Brendan. I'll eh, I'll just lash a bit of turf in that, will I?

FINBAR: Good man, Jim.

(Brendan gives Jim his drink. Jim leaves money on the bar and goes to the fireplace, leaving his drink on the mantel.)

JACK: Keep the chill out, ha?

FINBAR: This is it.

(Finbar looks at his watch.)

VALERIE: Do you want to?

FINBAR: Ah, no, no, no. I'm just watching the time. We've a wedding tomorrow.

VALERIE: Would you be . . . directly . . . working in the hotel?

JACK: Saves him paying someone's wages.

FINBAR: Sure that's how I have it, boy. *(He winks at Valerie)*

JACK: We know.

FINBAR: No there's certain things I do myself on a big day. One of the first things I ever learned in the business. The importance of good stock.

VALERIE: Soup stock?

FINBAR: For the soup. For the gravy, for the sauces, ah, you use it all over the place. And it's just a little thing I do. A little ritual. In the morning, I help do the stock. What do we have from yesterday and so on. A little mad thing I do, but there you are.

VALERIE: I think that's lovely.

FINBAR: Ah, it's a little thing I do. Little superstition. These'll tell you. I'm famous for it.

JACK: It's a gimmick.

BRENDAN: Who's geting married, Finbar?

FINBAR: Do you know Nuala Donnelly? "Nu" they call her. She used to work for me in the Arms. Declan Donnelly's girl. Gas young one.

BRENDAN: Oh yeah.

FINBAR: You used to be pals with Declan, Jim.

JIM: Poor Declan. Be dead ten years in July. God rest him. Lovely fella.

FINBAR: She's a gas young one, the daughter. "Nu" they call her. "Call me Nu," she says, the first day she was working for me. Not afraid to speak up for herself or anything. Used to tell us who was having affairs and all this. She was a chambermaid, you see. She knew the couples who were being all illicit because she'd go in to do the room in the morning and the bed would be already made. The woman in the affair would have done it out of guilt, you see. Cover it all up, for herself as much as for anyone else. She's a mad young one.

VALERIE: Would you get many people using the hotel like that?

FINBAR: Not at all. I wouldn't say so. But Nuala just, you know, she's a gabber and a talker.

JIM (At stove): Who's she getting married to, Finbar?

FINBAR: Oh Jesus, some fella from out the country. He must be in his forties. Shame, a young one getting hitched to an auldfella like that. He must have plenty of money. *(To Valerie, indicating Jack)* Be like getting married to that. He's a nice stash hidden away in that little garage, I'll tell you. Hoping to trap some little thing with it. Isn't that right, Jack?

JACK: That's my plan.

FINBAR: But you want to be careful of the old lads living on their own. They've a big pot of stew constantly on the heat, and they just keep throwing a few bits of scraps in it every couple of days. And they'd survive on that—don't you Jack? That'd do you?

JACK: It's a feast every day.

FINBAR: Aw. Dreadful fellas. And then they manage to get a girl and the dust'd be like that on everything. And your man'd be after living in two rooms all his life, and the poor young one would have to get in and clean it all out. Thirty years of old newspapers and cheap thrillers, all lying there in the damp since their mammies died and that was the last bit of cleaning went on in the place. That right Jack?

JACK: That's us to a tee.

BRENDAN: Jaysus, speak for yourself, ha?

FINBAR: Oh, they'd be desperate men. Changing the sheets in the bed every Christmas. And there'd be soot all over everything, and bits of rasher, and egg and pudding on the floor.

VALERIE: The poor girl.

JACK: Poor girl is right. So the least I can do is make sure her reception, in the Arms, is a little memory for her to have in the future, in the cold nights. Cheers.

(They have all enjoyed this.)

JACK: You've a terrible warped mind, do you know that?

FINBAR *(Winks at Valerie)*: Sure I'm only telling like it is, ha?

JIM: Nuala getting married. You don't feel the time.

FINBAR: No.

JIM: Mmm. I remember, oh, it must have been twenty or more years ago, doing a job with him. Declan. Talking about what we were saying earlier. The priest over in Glen was looking for a couple of lads to do a bit of work. And he was down in Carrick in the Arms. He'd, come over, from Glen, you know? Which was an odd thing anyway. Like what was he doing coming all the way over just to get a couple of young fellas? But Declan, Donnelly, got put on to him. There was a few quid and he knocked up to me and we were to go over to the church in Glen the following day. And I remember I was dying with the flu and I had a terrible high temperature. The mother was telling me to stay in the leaba. Burn it off. But like it was a couple of quid on the QT so I told Declan yeah, I'd do it tomorrow. No problem.

And then the next day it was lashing rain. I'll never forget it. He called for me in his dad's car. The smell of sheep in it like you wouldn't believe. God it would kill you. He used to put them in the car, chauffeur them around, you know?

(Smiles.)

And we drove over to Glen. And the priest took us into the sacristy, and the job, of all things was to dig a grave in the yard. That day was the removal of the remains and they needed the grave for the morning. And fair dues, like, Declan said it to him. Was there no one else around the place could have done it? And the priest got a bit cagey and he was saying something about the local boys being busy with a game of Gaa, or something. And the rain was pelting down and he gave us leggings and wellies and the whole bit they had there and a couple of shovels.

And then he put up his umbrella all annoyed, like, and he brought us out, over to a grave under a tree. It was a family one and there were two down in it already, the mother and the father and this was going to be for the boy. Well he was a man, like, a middle-aged fella. But there was two in it so we weren't going to have to go down for miles, like. So he went off to do his business and get ready, and me and Declan got stuck in. And with the rain and all, I was dying with the flu. My arms were sore and then my legs got sore. And then my neck got sore. And I was boiling. But we got down two, two and a half foot and we took a break. We got in Declan's car and he pulled out a bottle of poitín and a few sambos. I couldn't eat but I took a good belt of the bottle, like. Knocked me into some sort of shape. And we just sat there for a while, listening to the radio, and the rain coming down, and then we got out and got stuck in again. Having a little swig every half hour or so, keeping it going.

And we saw the hearse arrive then. And the mad thing was, there was only two or three other fellas there for the service. Of course the removal is only a short thing mostly, but to have no one there, and for a man who's not an old man, it was funny, you know?

And then that was over and the priest came out to us. We were nearly finished. And he just cleared us for the funeral in the morning, and then he went off. So me and Declan were the only two there, then. *(Short pause)* And your man was laid out in the church. And Declan went off to get a tarp to stretch over . . . the . . . grave, and I put a big lump of a door over it. And I was just waiting on Declan and having the last drop, under the tree and thinking we might stick the head in somewhere for a quick pint on the way back. You know?

And then I saw this, fella, come out of the church and he walked straight over to me. He was in a suit so I reckoned he was paying his respects or whatever. And over he comes, through the gravestones. And he was looking around him a bit, like he didn't know the place. And he stood beside me, under the tree, looking at the grave. I didn't know what to say, you know? And he goes, "Is this for so and so?" I forget the name. And I go, "That's right, yeah." And he says, "That's the wrong grave." And I'm like, "No. This is where the priest said, like." And he looked at me, breathing hard through his nose. Like he was holding his temper. And he goes, "Come on, I'll show you." And he walks off.

And I was all like "fuck this" you know? And I was cursing Declan, waiting for him to come back. And your man turns around, you know, "Come on, it's over here." I just, he was a loolah, you know? And I was nearly climbimg into the grave myself, with the tiredness. And I was sick. So I followed him just to get it over with. And he stopped at a grave. Like a new enough one. A white one with a picture of a little girl on it.

And he says, "It's this one here." And I just went, "Okay, right you are, Mister, I'll have it done, no problem. See you now." And he . . . sort of touched the gravestone and he went off, back into the church. I was breathing a few sighs of relief I'll tell you. And Declan came back with the tarp and I said, "Did you see your man?" And he didn't know what I was talking about. So I told him and all this, and we just kind of had a bit of a laugh at it. And we just got out of there. Stopped in the Green Man on the way back for a few pints and that night my fever broke. But I was knackered. The mother wouldn't let me go to the burial. Declan did it on his own I think. But I was laid up for a couple of days. And one day the mother brought me in the paper and on the obituaries, there was a picture of your man whose grave we'd dug. And you know what I'm going to say. It was the spit of your man I'd met in the graveyard. So I thought first it was a brother or a relative or someone, I'd met.

And I forgot about it a bit and didn't think about it for ages until one night Declan told me he'd found out why the priest from Glen was looking for a couple of Carrick fellas, for the job. The fella who'd died had had a bit of a reputation for em . . . being a pervert. And Jesus, when I heard that, you know? If it was him. And he wanted to go down in the grave with the . . . little girl. Even after they were gone. It didn't bear . . . thinking about. It came back when you said about Declan's girl. Yeah.

(*Pause.*)

FINBAR: Jaysus, Jim. That's a terrible story, to be telling.

JIM: Well, you know. And we'd been having the few little drinks. From Dick Lenihan's batch, you know?

JACK: Oh Jesus. Firewater. Sure that'd put a hole in the glass, let alone give you hallucinations.

(*A little laugh. Pause.*)

VALERIE: Do you think it was a, an hallucination Jim?

JIM: God, I don't know. I was flying like, but it was a right fluke him showing me where he wanted to be buried and me knowing nothing about him like.

VALERIE: Mm. (*Nods*)

FINBAR: Are you alright, Valerie? (*Little laugh*) You look a bit peaky there.

VALERIE: No, I'm fine. Just, actually, is the ladies out this way?

BRENDAN: Ah. (*Short pause*) Jays, I'll tell you what, Valerie, this is very embarrassing but the ladies is busted. And with the . . .

(*Jack laughs. Brendan chuckles a little.*)

I'm getting it fixed for the Germans like, but I haven't done it yet.

FINBAR: Ah, you're a terrible man, Brendan.

BRENDAN: No, I'll bring you in the house, come on.

VALERIE: Are you sure?

BRENDAN: Aw yeah, yeah, no problem.

JACK: Don't worry Valerie, if you're not back in ten minutes we'll come and get you, okay?

BRENDAN: Jaysus. Give it a rest. Come on Valerie, I'll put the lights on for you. Out this way.

FINBAR: Bye now.

VALERIE: Bye.

(Brendan, a little awkwardly, shepherds Valerie out the back. Pause.)

JACK: Yep.

(Short pause.)

FINBAR *(To Jim)*: Jaysus. That's some fucking story. To be telling a girl, like. Perverts out in the country. For fuck's sake.

(Short pause.)

JACK: Like your story had nothing in it, ha?

FINBAR: Ah that was only old headers in it.

JACK: But you brought the whole thing up. With the fairies. The fairies! She's in that house.

FINBAR: I forgot it was that house. I forgot it was Maura Nealon. It was an honest mistake.

JACK: Honest mistake.

FINBAR: What.

JACK: Don't be giving it that old cod now.

FINBAR: What do you mean?

JACK: With bringing her around and all.

FINBAR: What about it?

JACK: Bringing her up the Head and all.

(Short pause. Finbar looks at Jim and back at Jack.)

FINBAR: Yeah?

JACK: So don't be giving it the old cod now.

FINBAR: What cod, Jack? *(Pause)* I'm asking you. *(Short pause)*
What?

JIM: Ah boys, we have a small one. Come on now.

FINBAR: Hang on a minute, Jim. What?

JACK: Well you get me to tell a story about the house she's in.

FINBAR: I didn't know that though. I told you that.

JACK: Whatever. And then you tell the story about the
Walsh girl.

FINBAR: Sure it was you told me to say that.

JACK: What?

FINBAR: Talking about the fags and giving up the fags and
all that. When you offered them that time.

JACK: Would you cop on? Ghosts and "Giving up the fags."

FINBAR: Okay. I'm sorry. What? I regret the stories, then. I
don't think we should have anymore of them. But
that's what I'm saying, like.

JIM: I didn't think. I just said it. With, Declan Donnelly and
that. It just, you know . . .

FINBAR: Ah no no no. Jim. We're not blaming anybody. I
regret it now. And let's not have any more of them,
and that's all.

JACK: Oh you regret it now?

FINBAR: Yeah.

JACK: It's not part of the tour.

FINBAR: Ah now, come on.

JACK: Bit of local color.

FINBAR: No. Jack.

JACK: Just don't berate Jim for telling a story after you
telling one yourself.

FINBAR: I apologize, if that's what I did. Sorry Jim. Now, I'll
say that. But stop with this . . . tour-guide thing. That's
not fair. The woman's moved out here on her own. For
some reason. There's something obviously going on . . . in

her life. I'm just trying to make it easier for her. Give her a welcome, for fuck's sake. So don't . . . be implying anything else. I don't like it. *(Pause)* I've apologized to Jim. And I'm saying no more stories. *(Short pause)* Sure I'm married! I mean really. Yous are the single boys. *(Short pause. Warm)* Sure I can't remember the last time I saw a suit on you.

(Pause.)

JACK: Oh now it's me?

JIM: Ah now boys, come on. That's enough. That's enough of that.

JACK: You think I have intentions, is it?

FINBAR: I don't know. You're entitled.

JACK: I do often wear a suit. Don't come in here for the first time in God knows, thinking we're fucking hicks. 'Cause you're from round here.

(Pause.)

FINBAR: Nobody's saying that. You've got the wrong idea, Jack. And it's not worth falling out over. Now, I'll buy you a drink. And that'll be the fucking end of it now. Alright?

JACK: You will not buy me a fucking drink. *(Short pause)* I'll buy *you* one, and *that'll* be the end of it.

(Jack extends his hand. They shake.)

JIM: That's more like it, men. That's more like it, ha?

(Jack goes in behind the bar.)

JACK: What'll yous have?

FINBAR *(Offering hand to Jim)*: Sorry Jim.

JIM: Ah no no no. Stop. *(Shaking hands)* It's forgotten.

JACK: Finbar.

FINBAR: Ah. I think I'll just have a glass, Jack, I think.

JACK: Ah, you'll have a small one with that.

FINBAR: Jays, you'll fucking kill me now, ha? I think he's trying to kill me Jim, is he?

JIM: Oh now.

JACK: Jim?

JIM: Small one, Jack, thanks.

JACK: You'll have a little pint with that I think.

JIM: Go on, ha?

FINBAR: Ah good man. *(Pause)* Jays. That was a hot one there for a minute, ha?

JACK: We'll say no more about it. We might tell a few jokes when she comes back.

(They laugh.)

FINBAR: Jays. This is it. How's the mammy, Jim?

JIM: Ah, do you know what it is? She's just old. And everything's going on her.

FINBAR: Ah Jaysus, ha? I'll have to get up and see her.

JACK: I was saying that earlier. It'd be the time, you think, Jim.

JIM: Ah.

FINBAR: She does be alright on her own, with coming out for an old jar or that.

JIM: Oh don't mind her. She's well able to tell you what's what. The only thing would be the eyes. But she's the one. I'm always mixing up the tablets. She knows exactly what she's supposed to be taking when. So. But we have the telly in that room. And she'll listen to that and drop off.

FINBAR: Well that's alright, isn't it.

JIM: Oh she's still . . . I'm taking her over to see her sister in the, in the order.

JACK: That's a closed order, Jim, yeah?

JIM: Yeah, you know. They don't talk and all that. But the sister is six years older than the mammy, now, you know, so . . .

FINBAR: Gas. She'll be alright for the drive?

JIM: Oh, she'll be knackered, she'll be out like a light when we get back.

FINBAR: Ah.

JIM: Ah yeah.

(Brendan and Valerie come back.)

BRENDAN: So this was all the original. Before the house.

VALERIE: Right.

FINBAR: There you are, we thought we were going to have to send out a search party.

VALERIE: I was having a good nosy around.

FINBAR: Wasn't too much of a state, no?

VALERIE: Tidier than I normally am.

JACK: That's he had the sisters over today. That's all that is.

FINBAR: I saw them having their lunch in my place today.

BRENDAN: Don't be talking.

FINBAR *(Gingerly)*: Oh . . . back off there. Sensitive area. Eh, Valerie, darling, I don't want you to be stranded here with me now if I'm keeping you.

BRENDAN: Sure we can look after her.

FINBAR: Ah no, I'm grand for a while yet.

VALERIE: I, em. Hearing about. All these . . . you know, stories. It's . . .

FINBAR: Ah that's the end of them, now. We've had enough of them old stories, they're only an old cod. We've just been joking about it there when you were out. We'll all be all be witless, ha? We won't be able to sleep in our beds!

VALERIE: No, see, something happened to me. That just hearing you talk about it tonight. It's important to me. That I'm not . . . bananas.

I mean, I'm a fairly straight . . . down the line . . . person. Working. I had a good job at DCU. I had gone back to work after having my daughter, Niamh. My husband teaches, engineering, at DCU. We had Niamh in 1988. And I went back to work when she was five, when she started school. And we'd leave her with Daniel's parents, my husband's parents. His mother always picked her up from school. And I'd collect her after work. And last year she, she was dying to learn how to swim.

And the school had a thing. They'd take the class down to the CRC in Clontarf on Wednesdays. She was learning very well. No problem. Loved the water. She couldn't wait for Wednesdays and swimming. Daniel used to take her to the pool on Saturdays and everything.

But for such a bright, outgoing, happy girl she was a big em . . . She had a problem sleeping at night. She was afraid of the dark. She never wanted you to leave the room.

One of us would have to lie there with her until she went off, and even when she did, she'd often have to come in and sleep with us.

And I'd say to her, "What's wrong, when you go to bed?" But in the daytime, you know, she wouldn't care. Nighttime was a million miles away. And she wouldn't . . . think about it. But at night . . . there were people at the window, there were people in the attic, there was someone coming up the stairs. There were children knocking, in the wall. And there was always a man standing across the road who she'd see. Like there was loads of things. The poor . . . I wanted to bring her to the doctor, but Daniel said she'd grow out of it. And we should be careful, just, about books we got her, and what she saw on the telly and all of this.

But I mean, she used to even be scared that when she got up in the morning that Mammy and Daddy would have gone away and she'd be in the house on her own. That was one she told Daniel's mother. And all the furniture and carpets and everything would be gone. I mean, you know? So I told her after that, you know, we'd never, you know, it was ridiculous. And that if she was worried at all during the day to ring me, and

I'd come and get her, and there was nothing to worry about. And she knew our number, she was very good at learning numbers off and everything. She knew ours and her nana's and mine at work. She knew them all.

But then, in March, last year, the school had a, a sponsored swim, and the kids were going to swim a length of the pool. And I promised I was going to watch her. But I got . . . I was late, out of work, and I was only going to be in time to meet her afterwards, but em, when I got there . . . There was an ambulance and I thought, like, the pool is in the Central Remedial Clinic, so I thought like it was just somebody being dropped there. I didn't really pay any attention.

But when I got in, I saw that there was no one in the pool and one of the teachers was there with a group of kids. And she was crying and some of the children were crying. And this woman, another one of the mums came over and said there'd been an accident. And Niamh had hit her head in the pool and she'd been in the water and they'd been trying to resuscitate her. But she said she was going to be alright.

And I didn't believe it was happening. I thought it must have been someone else. And I went into, I was brought into, a room and Niamh was on a table. It was a table for table tennis, and an ambulance man was giving her the . . . kiss of life.

She was in her bathing suit. And the ambulance man said he didn't think what he was doing was work-ing. And he didn't know if she was alive. And he wrapped her in a towel and carried her out to the ambulance. And I got in the back with him. And they radioed on ahead, they were going to put her on a machine in Beaumont and try to revive her there. But the ambulance man knew, I think. She wasn't breath-ing, and he just knew, and he said if I wanted to say good-bye to her in the ambulance in case I didn't get a chance at the hospital.

And I gave her a little hug. She was freezing cold. And I told her Mammy loved her very much. She just looked asleep but her lips were gone blue and she was dead.

And it had happened so fast. Just a few minutes. And I don't think I have to tell you. How hard it was. Between me and Daniel, as well. It didn't seem real. At the funeral I just thought I could go and lift her out of the coffin and that would be the end of all this.

I think Daniel was. I don't know if he actually, blamed me, there was nothing I could do. But he became very busy in his work. Just. Keeping himself . . . em. But I was, you know, I was more, just I didn't really know what I was doing. Just walking around, wanting to . . . Sitting in the house, with Daniel's mother, fussing around the place.

Just, months of this. Not really talking about it, like.

(*Pause.*)

But, and then one morning. I was in bed, Daniel had gone to work. I usually lay there for a few hours, trying to stay asleep, really. I suppose. And the phone rang. And I just left it. I wasn't going to get it. And it rang for a long time. Em, eventually it stopped, and I was dropping off again. But then it started ringing again, for a long time. So I thought it must have been Daniel trying to get me. Someone who knew I was there.

So I went down and answered it. And. The line was very faint. It was like a crossed line. There were voices, but I couldn't hear what they were saying. And then I heard Niamh. She said, "Mammy?" And I . . . just said, you know, "Yes."

(*Short pause.*)

And she said . . . She wanted me to come and collect her. I mean, I wasn't sure whether this was a dream or

her leaving us had been a dream. I just said, "Where
are you?"

And she said she thought she was at Nana's. In the
bedroom. But Nana wasn't there. And she was scared.
There were children knocking in the walls and the
man was standing across the road, and he was looking
up and he was going to cross the road. And would I
come and get her?

And I said I would, of course I would. And I
dropped the phone and I ran out to the car in just a T-
shirt I slept in. And I drove to Daniel's mother's house.
And I could hardly see, I was crying so much. I mean,
I knew she wasn't going to be there. I knew she was
gone. But to think wherever she was . . . that . . . And
there was nothing I could do about it.

Daniel's mother got a doctor and I . . . slept for a
day or two. But it was . . . Daniel felt that I . . . needed
to face up to Niamh being gone. But I just thought
that he should face up to what happened to me. He
was insisting I get some treatment, and then . . . everything would be okay. But you know, what can help
that, if she's out there? She still . . . she still needs me.

(Pause.)

JACK: You don't think it could have been a dream you were
having, no?

(Short pause.)

VALERIE: I heard her.

(Short pause.)

FINBAR: Sure, you were after getting a terrible shock,
Valerie. These things can happen. Your . . . brain is trying to deal with it, you know? *(Pause)* Is your husband
going to . . . come down?

VALERIE: I don't think so.

FINBAR: Ah, it'd be a terrible shame if you don't . . . if you didn't see . . . him because of something as, as, you know . . . that you don't even know what it was.

(Short pause.)

BRENDAN: She said she knew what it was.

FINBAR: But sure you can't just accept that, that you, you know . . . I mean . . . surely you, you have to look at the broader thing of it here.

JIM: It might have been a wrong number.

BRENDAN: What?

JIM: It could have been a wrong number or something wrong with the phone, you know? And you'd think you heard it. Something on the line.

BRENDAN: But you wouldn't hear someone's voice on the fucking thing, Jim.

JIM: Just it might have been something else.

JACK: Here, go easy, Brendan, Jim's only trying to talk about the fucking thing.

FINBAR: Ah lads.

JACK: Just take it easy.

VALERIE: Stop. I don't want . . . It's something that happened. And it's nice just to be here and . . . hear what you were saying. I know I'm not crazy.

(Short pause.)

FINBAR: Valerie, love, nobody's going to think that. But . . . just . . . no one knows about these things, sure, they're not real even. You hear all sorts of old cod, all around. But there's usually some kind of explanation for it. Sure, Jim said himself he was delirious with the flu that time. Jim.

JIM: I had a right temperature.

FINBAR: Maura . . . eh . . . Nealon, sure she was in here every night of the week. Brendan. About how much would she drink? Be honest now.

BRENDAN: How much did she drink?

JACK: Have a bit of respect, Finbar.

FINBAR: I'm trying to make a point, Jack. The woman was a drinker.

JACK: We're all drinkers.

FINBAR: But, come on. She was an alcoholic, Valerie. She used to have a bottle of whiskey put away before you knew where you were. Sure who wouldn't be hearing knocking after that?

JACK: Ah you're not being fair on her now. The woman's dead, she can't defend herself.

FINBAR: I'm not casting anything on her. If she came in that door right now, if she was alive, I'd be buying her drink, and more power to her, I'd hope she'd enjoy it. I'd be the first to buy her a drink. But I run a bar myself down in the Arms. And I know all about what a right few drinks'll do to you. She liked her drop is what I'm saying.

BRENDAN: What about you? And the Walshes?

FINBAR: Look. How many times do I have to say it? They were all a bunch of fucking headbangers!

(Pause.)

I got the wind put up me that night. Fair enough. But that's what these stories do. But I resent that now. What I went through that night. But I was only young. And that's over with, fucking headbangers.

(Pause.)

And after all that, I'm ignoring the bigger thing. I'm very sorry about your daughter, Valerie, I'm very sorry indeed.

JACK: Oh we all are. Of course we are. It's terrible.

(*Long pause.*)

FINBAR (*Checks watch*): I'm going to have to go, I'm afraid. I
   don't want to, but . . .

VALERIE: Okay.

BRENDAN: Ah here, I'll leave her down.

FINBAR: But you might want to come on now, no?

VALERIE: Em.

BRENDAN: Ah, have another drink and relax for a little while.

VALERIE: Yeah, I think I'm going to hang on for another
   little while.

FINBAR: Are you going to go easy on the old stories?

JACK: Ah stop being an old woman. She'll be grand.

FINBAR: Alright?

JACK: She'll be grand.

JIM: Could I get a lift, Finbar?

FINBAR: Of course you can, Jim.

JACK: You're okay for Father Donal's car in the morning.

JIM (*Counting money*): No problem. I'll be there about quarter
   to nine.

JACK: Grand, just, I've got to get out to Conor Boland.

JIM: Yeah. It's fine. Brendan, em . . .

BRENDAN: Naggin'?

JIM: Please.

(*Brendan puts a small bottle of whiskey in a plastic bag and gives it to
Jim. Jim attempts to pay for it. Brendan discreetly waves him away.*)

FINBAR: Yep.

JIM: Well. Valerie.

VALERIE: It was very nice to meet you.

JIM (*Taking her hand*): I'm very sorry about what's happened
   to you. And I'm sure your girl is quite safe and comfortable wherever she is, and I'm going to say a little
   prayer for her, but I'm sure she doesn't need it. She's a

saint. She's a little innocent. And that fella I saw in the churchyard that time was only the rotten poitín and the fever I had. Finbar's right. You enjoy your peace and quiet here now. And we'll see you again. You're very nice. Good night now.

VALERIE: Good night. Thanks Jim.

JIM: That's alright.

FINBAR: Valerie. *(He takes her hand)*

VALERIE: Thanks for everything.

FINBAR: My pleasure, darling. And I'll call up to you now in the next day or two, and . . . *(Nods at her)*

VALERIE: Fine.

FINBAR: And we'll make sure you're alright and you're settling in with us. You're very welcome.

(He kisses her awkwardly on the cheek.)

VALERIE: Thanks for everything, Finbar.

FINBAR: That's quite alright. Men.

JACK: Finbar.

FINBAR: I'll see you soon, I hope, Jack.

(They shake hands.)

Alright?

JACK: See you soon.

FINBAR: Brendan.

BRENDAN: Take it easy now, Finbar. Look after yourself.

FINBAR: I won't leave it so long next time.

BRENDAN: Okay.

JIM: Good night.

BRENDAN: Good night Jim.

VALERIE: See you soon.

JACK: See you in the morning.

JIM: Quarter to nine.

FINBAR: See yous now.

(Jim and Finbar leave.)

JACK: There you are now.

BRENDAN: Mm.

JACK: I'm sorry for snapping. That time.

BRENDAN: Ah no. Sure. I was . . .

VALERIE: I think it was my fault.

JACK: Would you go on? Of course it wasn't your fault. You know . . . It's all very well, us sitting around, fecking around with these old stories. But then, for something personal like that. That's happened to you. People are going to deal with it, in different ways. Jim, was, you know . . .

BRENDAN: Yeah . . .

JACK: He didn't mean anything.

BRENDAN: He didn't really mean there was anything wrong with your phone, I don't think.

(They laugh a little. Pause.)

JACK: It's em . . . a terrible thing that happened. Do you ever get over something like that, I wonder? I don't mean the phone . . . call, you know.

VALERIE: I know. *(Pause)* I don't know. *(Pause)*

JACK: We're very sorry.

BRENDAN: Come on, we sit near the stove. It's getting cold. We'll have a last one.

JACK: Good idea.

BRENDAN: Give us your glass, Valerie. Jack, you'll have a small one, for the road.

VALERIE: Can I get this?

JACK: Ah no no no.

BRENDAN: It's on the house now. Bar's officially closed. Go on.

(Jack and Valerie move nearer the stove.)

JACK: You get yourself in there now. We'll be grand in a minute.

BRENDAN: I'm going to give you a little brandy, Valerie. This
wine is freezing in the fridge.

JACK: Good man.

VALERIE: Oh lovely. Thanks.

JACK: Good girl. That's it now. *(To Brendan)* Jim'll be in a
bad way, all the same when the mammy goes, what do
you think Brendan?

BRENDAN: Oh definitely. She's been very sick, Valerie, for
years now. Fading fast, like, for years! She still spoils
that boy rotten, ha? Though.

JACK: Oh definitely. Oh yeah.

(Brendan brings the drinks over.)

VALERIE: That's an awful lot.

BRENDAN: Ah it's not really.

JACK: There's no law says you have to drink it all, ha? Your
man does put it back in the bottle.

BRENDAN: Would you ever fuck off?

JACK: I think we should drink this to you, sweetheart.

BRENDAN: Yes. To Valerie.

JACK: Hope it's all . . . *(Raises glass)* In the end . . .

BRENDAN: Cheers.

VALERIE: Cheers.

(They drink. Jack considers Brendan for a moment.)

JACK: There's the boy, ha?

(They smile.)

VALERIE: You've no children, Jack, no?

JACK: No, darling, never married. But I do be telling this
fella to be on the lookout. A youngfella like him. Not
to end up like me.

VALERIE: Do you wish you had married?

JACK: Sure who'd have me? A cantankerous old fucker like me.

BRENDAN: Too right.

JACK: Yeah . . . It's a thing, you know? I do say it to
Brendan. I'm down in the garage. And the fucking tin
roof on the thing. On my own on that country road.
You see it was bypassed by the main road into Carrick.
And there's no . . . like in the summer the heat has the
place like an oven, with the roof, or if it's not that,
it's the rain pelting down on it like bricks, the noise of
it. And there you'll be, the only car stopping in be
someone that knows the area real well. Ah, you'd definitely feel it, like. But you know. I get down here for a
pint and that. There's a lot to be said for the company.
And the . . . you know, the . . . someone there. Oh
yeah.

VALERIE: Did you never consider it? When you were young.

JACK: Oh sure. Yeah. Of course I did. Sure what the hell
else does a youngfella be thinking about? You know?

And Brendan knows. I had a girl. A lovely girl back
then. We were courting for three, years, and em . . .
1963 to '66. But she wanted to go up to Dublin, you
know. She would have felt that's what we should have
done. And I don't know why it was a thing with me
that I . . . an irrational fear, I suppose, that, kept me
here. And I couldn't understand why she wanted to be
running off up to Dublin, you know? And she did in
the end, anyway, like. And she was working up there
waiting for me to come.

But with me it was a mad thing, that I thought it
was a thousand fucking miles away. Hated going up.

I went up a few times like. But . . . I was going up
for . . . you know . . . she had a room. A freezing, damp
place. I was a terrible fella. It became that that was the
only thing I was going for. I couldn't stand being away.
I don't know why. Ah, I'd be all excited about going up
for the physical . . . the freedom of it. But after a day
and a night, and I'd had my fill, we'd be walking in the
park and I'd be all catty and bored, and moochy.

(Pause.)

Breaking the poor girl's heart. Ah, you get older and look back on why you did things, you see that a lot of the time, there wasn't a reason. You do a lot of things out of pure cussedness.

I stopped answering her letters. And I'd fucking dread one coming to the house. And her in it wondering how I was and was there something wrong with the post or this.

(Pause.)

I can't explain what carry on I was up to. I had just . . . left her out. Being the big fella, me dad handing over the business to me. Me swanning around. A man of substance. And then I had the gall to feel resentful when she wrote and said she was getting married to a fella.

(Pause.)

And I was all, that it was her fault for going up in the first place. Tss.

There was a delegation of people from all around here going up to the wedding on a bus. And I was just one of the crowd. Just one of the guests. In my suit, and the shoes nearly polished off me. And a hangover like you wouldn't believe. I'd been up till five or more, swilling this stuff, looking at the fire. And we were all on the bus at nine. And all the chat all around was why she hadn't come home to get married. And me sick as a dog.

The smell of Brylcreem off all us culchies. Sitting in the church in Phibsboro. All her lovely-looking nurse friends and their guard boyfriends. She was marrying a guard. Huge fella. Shoulders like a big gorilla. And they were coming down the aisle after, and I caught her eye. And I gave her the cheesiest little grin you've ever seen. A little grin that was saying, "Enjoy your big gorilla, 'cause the future's all ahead of me."

And she just looked at me like I was only another guest at the wedding. And that was that. And the future was all ahead of me. Years and years of it. I could feel it coming. All those things you've got to face on your own. All by yourself. And you bear it 'cause you're showing everybody that you're a great fella altogether.

But I left the church like a little boy. And I walked away. I couldn't go to the reception. I just kept walking. There was a light rain. I just kept walking. And then I was in town. It was a dark day. Like there was a roof on the city. And I found myself in a little labyrinth of streets. With nothing doing. And I ducked into a pub. Little, dark place. Just one or two others there. A businesslike barman. Like yourself Brendan, ha?

Businesslike, dutiful. And I put a pint or two away. And a small one or two. And I sat there, just looking down at the dirty wooden bar. And the barman asked me if I was alright? Simple little question. And I said I was. And he said he'd make me a sandwich. And I said okay. And I nearly started crying—because, you know, here was someone just . . . and I watched him.

He took two big slices off a fresh loaf and buttered them carefully, spreading it all around. I'll never forget it. And then he sliced some cheese and cooked ham and an onion out of a jar, and put it all on a plate and sliced it down the middle. And, just someone doing this for me. And putting it down in front of me. "Get that down you now," he said. And then he folded up his newspaper and put on his jacket and went off on his break. And there was another barman then.

And I took this sandwich up and I could hardly swallow it, because of the lump in my throat. But I ate it all down because someone I didn't know had done this for me. Such a small thing. But a huge thing in my condition. It fortified me, like no meal I ever had in my life. And I went to the reception. And I was properly ashamed of myself. There was a humility I've tried to find since. But goodness wears off. And it just gets easier to be a contrary bollocks.

Down in the garage. Spinning small jobs out all day. Taking hours to fix a puncture. Stops you thinking about what might have been and what you should have done. It's like looking away. Like I did at that reception. You should only catch someone's eye for the right reason. And I'll tell you—there's not one morning I don't wake up with her name in the room. (*Pause*) And I do be at this fella. Don't I? (*Pause*) Yep. (*Pause*) I may be on my way now.

BRENDAN: Will you be okay in that wind?

JACK: Jaysus, I should be used to that road by now, says you, ha?

BRENDAN: I'll get you the torch.

JACK: Am I a moaner?

BRENDAN (*Going*): There's well fucking worse, I'll tell you. (*Exits*)

JACK: Well. That wasn't a ghostly story. Anyway. At least, ha?

VALERIE: No.

JACK: We've had enough of them. (*Pause*) We'll all be ghosts soon enough, says you, ha?

VALERIE: Mmm.

JACK: We'll all be sitting here. Sipping whiskey all night with Maura Nealon. (*Pause*) Yeah. (*Short pause*) This has been a strange little evening for me.

VALERIE (*A little laugh*): For me as well.

JACK: Fuck. We could do worse. It was lovely to meet you.

VALERIE: You too.

JACK: I didn't mean to go on there.

VALERIE: No, please . . .

JACK: Something about your company. Inspiring, ha? And this of course. (*Glass*)

(They smile.)

I wonder if being out here in the country is the best place for you to . . . you know . . .

VALERIE: Why?

JACK: Ah. Girl like you. Hiding yourself away. Listening to old headers like us talking about the fairies. Having all your worst fears confirmed for you. Tuh. Ghosts and angels and all this? Fuck them. I won't have it. Because I won't see someone like you being upset by it. You've enough to . . . deal with, for fuck's sake. I am very, sorry, love, about what happened.

VALERIE: Thanks.

(Brendan comes in turning the torch on and off.)

BRENDAN: The batteries are a bit weak. Come on, I'll drop you.

JACK: Are you sure?

BRENDAN: Sure, I'm giving Valerie a lift.

VALERIE: Come with us.

JACK: Okay, then. Grand.

(Brendan is clearing glasses, going in behind the bar, tidying up.)

VALERIE: Do you want a hand, Brendan?

BRENDAN: Oh no! Stay where you are, I'll be finished in a sec.

(Jack takes his anorak, joking.)

JACK: Is this yours, Valerie?

VALERIE: Yeah right.

(Jack takes her jacket and holds it for her to put on.)

JACK: Come on.

VALERIE: Oh now. Very nice.

JACK: These are the touches, ha, Brendan?
BRENDAN: That's them.
JACK: Now.
VALERIE: Thanks.
JACK: Mmm. Have a last fag I think.

(Taking cigarette packet.)

Anyone else?
VALERIE: No, I won't thanks.
BRENDAN: No, I'm grand thanks, Jack.
JACK: Up early in the morning. Over to Conor Boland. He's
over the other side of Carrick there. Has about fifteen
fucking kids. Dirty bollocks.

(Brendan and Valerie laugh.)

And you should see her. Built like a fucking tractor.
The head on her.
BRENDAN: You're a terrible man.
JACK: I've had my moments.

(Brendan looks at Valerie and shakes his head.)

VALERIE: Will you be in here again soon?
JACK: Ah I'm always in and out. Got to keep the place
afloat at least, you know?
BRENDAN *(Working)*: Don't mind him now, Valerie. Him and
the Jimmy fella'll be fierce scarce around here the next
few weeks.
VALERIE: Why?
BRENDAN *(Stops work and lights a cigarette)*: All the Germans'll
be coming and they love it in here.
VALERIE *(To Jack)*: You don't like that?

(Jack makes a face.)

BRENDAN: He thinks they're too noisy.

JACK: See, you don't know what they do be saying or anything.

BRENDAN: Him and Jimmy be sitting there at the bar with big sour pusses on them. Giving out like a couple of old grannies.

JACK: Ah we're not that bad.

BRENDAN: You're like a pair of bloody auldones, you should see them.

VALERIE: Where do you go instead?

JACK: Ah, place down in Carrick, the Pot.

BRENDAN (*Derision*): "The Pot." There does be just as many of them down there don't be codding yourself.

JACK: Ah no, it doesn't seem as bad down there, now.

VALERIE: That's because this is your place.

JACK: Now. You've hit it on the head. You see, Brendan, Valerie's defending us. It's out of respect for this place.

BRENDAN: It is in my fucking barney respect! The two of yous leaving me standing behind that bar with my arms folded, picking my hole and not knowing what the hell is going on. And them playing all old sixties songs on their guitars. And they don't even know the words.

And nothing for me to do except pull a few pints and watch the shadow from the Knock moving along the floor, with the sun going down. I'm like some fucking mentler, I do be watching it! Watching it creeping up on the Germans. And they don't even notice it. I must be cracking up if that's my entertainment of an evening.

JACK: Ah don't be moaning. I'll tell you what. If Valerie's willing to come in and brave the Germans, then I'm sure me and Jim'll come in and keep yous company, hows that now?

BRENDAN: Oh you'll *grace* us with your ugly mushes, will you?

JACK: Don't push it, boy. Ah sure, Jaysus, what am I talking about? Sure you'll have Finbar in here sniffing around Valerie every night anyway.

VALERIE: Ah now stop.

(They laugh a little.)

JACK: He'll be like a fly on a big pile of shite, so he will.
    Jesus. That came out all wrong, didn't it?
BRENDAN: No Jack. That was perfect. As usual.
JACK: Couldn't have come out worse. Sorry about that.
VALERIE: Would you relax?

(Brendan is putting his jacket on.)

JACK: Sorry. Will you anyway?
VALERIE: What? Come in . . . with the . . . Germans?
JACK: Yeah.
VALERIE: Doesn't bother me.
JACK: Ah, I think that's the right attitude. You should stay
    with the company and the bright lights.
BRENDAN *(Looking around)*: Do you see my keys?

(Valerie and Jack look around a little bit.)

VALERIE: Sure I might even learn some German.
JACK: Ah, I don't know. They're eh . . . Are they from
    Germany, Brendan?
BRENDAN: What?
JACK: The Germans. *(To Valerie)* We call them the Germans.

(Valerie picks keys off the mantelpiece.)

VALERIE: Is this them?
BRENDAN: Yeah, thanks. Are we right?

(They are moving toward the door.)

JACK: Where are they from. Is it Denmark, or Norway? *(To Valerie)* It's somewhere like that.

(Jack goes out, followed by Valerie.)

BRENDAN: Ah I don't know where the fuck they're from.

(Brendan turns off the light and leaves. Slow fade.)

End of Play

ST. NICHOLAS

For Paddy Breathnach and Robert Walpole

And for Rionach

AUTHOR'S NOTE

Christmas for most of us can be very busy. Catching up with
friends in pubs for nights on end. It can become like work,
like this is your bizarre job. It involves meeting a lot of new
people too. Friends of friends. Sometimes it's nice and sometimes it's awkward. Last Christmas I decided to break the ice
by telling each new person I met a big lie. And this is it.

I was coming across the Ha'penny bridge today and a
seagull blew into my face. It got all tangled up in my glasses
and its wings were flapping around my head. People were
milling around, trying to help me, and I ended up lying on
the ground until they got it free. The seagull was fine and
so was I, but as you can imagine, it was very embarrassing.

The first thing people would say after I'd said this was,
"Is that true?" Because although they didn't believe me, we
live in a world where we don't expect complete strangers to
lie to us. Not in pubs at any rate. But it's nice in the theatre.

St. Nicholas is a play performed by one actor. He only
plays one character and he doesn't act anything out. He
just tells us a story. And for me, that's full of mischief.

When two or more actors talk to each other on stage, it's
easy for us to pretend they're not actually in the theatre. If
it's good they could be anywhere. Up a mountain, in a foot-
ball, under the sea, anywhere. But with one actor talking
only to the audience, what we have in front of us is a guide.
He's telling us about somewhere outside the theatre, not
trying to recreate it indoors. The theatre is simply where we
meet him. And if it's good, we're reminded that we are in
the theatre and we like being there.

And that's full of mischief because we collude with the actor in a very direct way. Especially when we have a well-known actor in front of us pretending to be someone else in a small theatre. It's a case of "Who's fooling who here?" And that can be a very rich and liberating experience. Because we've all started playing. It's a very grown-up and well-disciplined type of playing, granted, but then so are lots of things. Like making the character a theatre critic.

But just as children's playing is often a rehearsal for adult life and dealings, so our theatrical grown-up playing has its serious intents. Because we are reflective beings and we like neatness. We want to know what everything *means*. "What the hell am I supposed *to make* of this?"—that's us. That's what makes us responsible. And I think that's what *St. Nicholas* might be about. The responsibility reason gives us.

Conor McPherson,
JANUARY 1997

PRODUCTION HISTORY

St. Nicholas was first produced by the Bush Theatre, London,
on February 19, 1997. The lighting was by Paul Russell.
It was performed by Brian Cox and directed by Conor
McPherson. The production made its American debut
on March 11, 1998 at New York City's Primary Stages,
Casey Childs, Artistic Director; Deborah Constantine
was lighting designer.

CHARACTER AND PLACE

A MAN, late fifties

A bare stage.

PART ONE

When I was a boy, I was afraid of the dark . . . What was there.

And maybe one of the things I thought was there was vampires.

I don't know. I can't remember now.

But like all of us, whatever idea I did have about them, it was probably all the superstitious bullshit we get in books. And fiction. But that was nothing like the real thing. Like anything, the real thing is a lot more ordinary.

It's a "matter of fact." Matter of fact.

And that's far more frightening than anything you can make up.

Because it's real.

It's just there. Casual as everything else. Just waiting to be dealt with.

And there are practical things to be learned. Yes indeed.

Back in those days I was a fat bastard.

And I had a big red mush from drinking.

This is back before I met the vampires.

Before I knew what power was and what evil was.

But back then I thought I knew everything.

And I had lots of what I thought power was.

Because I was a theatre critic.

I was a journalist. I was a lucky bastard. I was blessed, or cursed, whichever, with the ability to string words together. I could string words together.

And that's all it was.

I mean, I was intelligent, but I had no real thoughts about things.

I'd never taken the care to form an opinion. I just had them.

And only one care in the world, when I think back on it now, me.

I wanted . . . everything.

Love, I suppose. Respect. Esteem.

But I didn't deserve it. No, I don't think I deserved any respect. But I got it.

Oh yeah. I got it. Because people were afraid of me. I loved it. Going to big productions. Big names.

Careers spanning tens of glittering years.

And everyone afraid of what I'd write?

Of what I "liked?"

And I hardly really liked anything.

And even when I did like something, mostly what I felt was . . . jealous.

I had tried writing.

Tried to convey the feelings I had.

That I genuinely fucking had—for people.

I loved people. I loved the stupid bastards.

But. I had no ideas.

No ideas for a story.

I wanted to let my compassion seep out across the stage.

Handicapped people in love.

Queers and lesbians absolving each other.

A liberal, fucking, all encompassing . . . you know.

But nothing came.

Nothing ever came.

I could only write about what there was already. I was a hack.
And I was drunk. I was at gallery openings, milling free
glasses of wine. I was in the bar after the premiere of plays.

I was the educated friend of the masses who read me.
Protecting them from these artistic charlatans who were
trying to rob their money.

And I could feel this . . . light. Going out. I could feel it.

It was panic I suppose.

Getting older, nothing done yet.

I started rows with directors in pubs.

I walked out of plays ten minutes before the end. I was on
the telly.

I had all this drive, going nowhere. It was putting me in the
ground.

And I'd get a fright you see. And I'd drink. And when I
drank I always got vicious hangovers. And I'd be useless.
Couldn't do a thing. Just do it again.

And you see, my life was quite conducive to that. There
wasn't a problem.

I only needed to get about one solid hour done in a day.
And then I was free.

I rehashed columns.

I usually had reviews written before the show was finished.

I could leaf through a current affairs magazine, see something, half an hour, I'd have a thousand words.

Tide me over.

And I was probably in the top five highest paid in the paper. You know? Editors licked the hole off me.

I was a character.

Famous in all the wrong ways. Nobody went without.

Not my fat tracksuit wife.

She didn't want anything.

She was happy enough to get a half bottle of gin into her.

And the days just slipped through her thick fingers.

Big house in the right place.

The cars and the cash. We were a pair of fat fuckers rolling around in the mud.

And our kids.

My girl was at college.

I loved her. I loved her in that way I couldn't look her in the eye, you know? I couldn't find the words.

It was too late. I just left money on the kitchen table every week.

Apparently she was a brilliant student, and I suspected she was a writer but I don't think I could have faced it if she was. You know? I avoided her.

I sat in my study with Milton and Chaucer, nice and cozy. And I'd finish a bottle and hit the sack at two or three.

And then I'd hear my boy come in.

He did nothing and I supported it.

All I knew was he stank of deodorant and he had some fruitless ambition to be a musician. Plinking away at that hour of the night.

He didn't want anything to do with me. And even now my face is burning when I think about my children.

And my stomach is like a brick wall.

Well I'd be too drunk to hear my wife snoring for long and I'd lie in the dark with morning coming.

She knew better than to try and touch me. And I would remember that I loved her once, when we were young. We used to sit in her house and everything outside was made for us. All we had to do was keep holding hands. And I couldn't even do that.

No, what I could do was sit in those yellow bars. With the journalists. Men falling in their pints. There was a breed of us, you see, and we weren't mere reporters.

We had columns.

There'd be a gang.

Men and women.

The women just on the verge of going to seed. Just on the brink, you understand.

And I was a big shot in those places. I could've had my pick.

I knew I could.

Those women with buckles on their shoes and their bows all done wrong.

They had each other, those journalists. There were one or two young things in the bloom of youth, but then the responsibility, you see, the responsibility got them. They were expected to have an opinion. On everything.

They were expected to be on top of situations and the current . . . goings on.

Otherwise, what justified their existence?

The man in the street needed to know what to think, hence these objective observers. And that may have partly been their fucking . . . thing.

But the other was the pressure to fill space. Just fill column inches. It's not a pleasant feeling.

You've got to fill it with words.

And these kids could never admit they couldn't find the news. They all used to rob each other.

They'd be dizzy for a year or two. All aflutter with responsibility.

And then all asunder with it.

And then the weight would pile on. Because there was a need for stimulation, wasn't there?

It became more and more that it was easier to stay in town than go home.

A few scoops at teatime.

And then, time to eat. Money to lose.

And, you fell in with another journalist, as a lover, you were a goner.

Because you'd help each other to keep going. And you'd look at each other with a joyous tear of camaraderie. And then a bawling hatred because . . . well, because you knew this was hell.

Of course it wasn't all like that.

Newspapers wouldn't get printed if it was. There wasn't many of us.

But enough. Enough drunken pig-headedness being passed off as authority.

That's the way I perceived it.

That was the world I was in.

Fuck. You think I was going to surround myself with people who were succeeding?

And what was I like in those places . . .

I wasn't dying, like you might think.

No. I was dead.

And every so often, I get it. I'd smell the rot. And the scotch'd start disappearing fairly fucking sharpish.

Mmm. I was a bollocks to all the other critics.

And I'll tell you why, because it was this: they were all cunts.

Well. I couldn't stand their wishy-washiness. They were always looking for an angle. Like children jumping up behind each other to see a parade.

Like the kids filling space.

But most of all I hated them because I wanted them to like me.

But all I was good at was being noticed. The only way I knew how.

By being . . . well, I'd never sit beside another critic.

All that effort being put into being . . . a type of thing.

I had none left for at home.

I would wake up and "do some work."

Do an hour.

And my wife would make some lunch for me. And she would sit with me.

She wanted me to say something.

And I could taste her care.

And I'd munch it down.

What are you going to do?

You've got to keep it in, haven't you?

You open those floodgates, Christ knows what the hell is going to come pouring out.

So, it was into town. Stick the head in the office. A few likely recruits.

And a quick jaunt down to wherever the fuck you reckoned you weren't going to be poisoned by the beer.

And I think we took comfort from being in those places.

Where at one time, genius was at work. Or play or . . . Kavanagh, O'Nolan, and what have you.

You know, that it was still possible to produce enduring works even though you were hungover or drunk, even. And then you began to think that it was the only way to produce enduring works.

But, there was nothing noble about those writers waking up at dawn, pissed out of their bins, groping around for the bottle they'd taken home, putting their hand in the puke that had finally let them sleep.

But we'd keep it up . . . all this.

Until nobody really fucking cared anymore.

And then I'd shoot off down to the Project or the Peacock to witness another amateur disaster.

And on, and on, and on.

But this was before I met the vampires. Before I worked for them.

Before I had to fight for anything.

It was a girl that got me into trouble.

Unintentionally. It was my fault.

She was an up-and-coming actress.

I was reviewing a new production of *Salome* at the Abbey.

And when she danced. Fuck me.

I mean, shadows crept about the muscles of her legs. Her arms. Even her fingers had such . . . She was just one more fucking . . . thing beyond my reach.

But I had underestimated my reviewing . . . capacity.

One of my very few moments of modesty.

Back in those days.

It was after the show in the Flowing Tide.

I'd made it for last orders.

My review was already phoned in.

I'd written it on the back of my program during the show.

Then I rang it in from my car.

And that was the end of that. That was the way I did it.

It was the best of everything.

I could stand there with the cast and ruin their evening. And get paid for it.

I was feeling generous that night.

I gave them a mixed review.

It was twenty past when I got to the pub.

I got two pints and two double Jemmies.

Now I could relax.

I knew Peter Hamilton, the director, from a few years before when I'd been speaking at a symposium on Irish theatre.

He was a prick.

He came over to me.

The cast were mostly in one corner.

I saw the actress who'd played Salome.

Her name was Helen.

I saw her glance over.

Hamilton said he was surprised to see me there. "Why?" I said.

I had no time for him.

But plenty of time to make that clear, if you know what I mean.

"Were you not reviewing us tonight?" he said. Awful high-pitched voice.

I told him the review was gone in, and if he nipped over to the paper he could probably get tomorrow's edition.

"Ah, no rush," he said.

But I could see him getting a little bit restless.

He had no cop.

I knew he was going to give in and ask me. And he did.

"If it's already gone in," he said, "you might as well tell me what you thought."

And then he gave a little laugh like none of this mattered, and he took a big gulp from his pint.

"What I thought," I said.

I was pretending I'd given it so much consideration it was hard to sum up now.

"Yes," I said. "Well I think it's one of the best shows I've seen in years and anybody who knows what's what would be a fool to miss it."

Well. Hamilton could hardly contain himself. He made the effort to stick around and make a bit of chitchat with me, but as soon as he got the chance he shot off to tell the others.

And that's how the party got going.

A kind of euphoria spread quite quickly and even the barmen didn't seem to want to stop serving.

I got chatting to the cast.

Drinks were placed in front of me.

I even began to believe my own hype. I began to think I had given it a good review.

I was walking around congratulating everybody. "My life has been changed," I told them.

They hugged me and I wept.

Why I wept I don't know.

Just an accumulation of drink and aggravated lying, I suppose, but I did.

And it worked and they all thought I was great.

I was different from the other critics who didn't know what they were talking about.

I had a passionate belief in the theatre and what makes it good.

And then we were out in the street and I was tired.

They wanted to go on somewhere else but I knew I was finished.

And anyway, it was only a matter of time before someone got their hands on the paper and saw what a lying bastard I was.

I leaned against the car and bid them good night.

And off they went.

And then, a cool hand.

Helen.

"I think I'll go home as well," she said.

I asked her where she lived.

Donnybrook. It was on my way.

Next thing, she was sitting beside me and we were driving through the empty streets.

You know that way?

And I couldn't help taking a sneaky look at her legs.

And I drove fairly slowly.

We didn't talk.

I badly, badly wanted to tell her the truth.

But I wasn't able to.

This was my moment and . . . I may never be that close to her again.

You know?

When we'd stop at the lights and this, I'd be giving her friendly . . . you know? Smiling at her.

Chaucer and Milton were in the back of the car. Having a great fucking time.

But this was just a lift home.

Let's not get excited.

Dropped her off in Pembroke Park.

She kissed me on the cheek before she got out. And I was the lowest thing.

"Good luck tomorrow night," I said.

And she told me to sleep well.

I couldn't sleep.

I sat in my study with the windows open. That summer breeze.

And I thought about killing myself. I could imagine the cast reading the review I'd actually given them, talking about what a complete cunt I was. And then they'd find out I was dead and they'd feel rotten. That they hadn't taken into account the integrity you know? The mystery that I was. But I was too chicken for that.

Instead I lay on the sofa and things crawled all over me till it got bright.

Well. I wasn't the same after that.

The summer, all our prospects, that bright youthful . . .

I was hacking away, reviewing books. On the radio, what have you.

And I couldn't stop thinking about her. I'd be working and suddenly I'd remember her and be all . . . fucking hell.

Happy. But that tinge as well.

Wasn't a sexual thing.

If she were ever to give herself to me, it'd be her acceptance of me. My fat, blotchy skin wasn't the point.

I don't think I even wanted that.

I knew that when we were married, I'd be happy enough just to sit and watch her tend our beautiful children.

Yeah.

Well the show didn't get any good reviews as it turned out, but the news was it was doing two weeks in London, knocked down from an intended four.

I went back to the Abbey the night it closed.

Broke my fucking heart to watch her.

And I'll tell you, because it was in her arms.

Because you could see her arms working. The weight changing there.

With you and me, it's all this:

We get older, we try to hide the excess. We compensate for our appearance with our "sense of humor" or our taste, or our . . . mind.

But what if you woke up in the morning and you were the physical specimen you always wanted to be.

Wouldn't that make you happy? Of course it would.

Go a long way in any case.

Because now your smile would beam confidence. Your stride would never need to conceal the way you were built.

And we could all concentrate on just being nice to each other.

This is all getting very nazi now. But Helen had that.

She was never conscious of herself, because everybody else was busy doing that for her. Do you see?

You probably don't.

But that's why when she smiled at you, you knew you were blessed because her will was pure. She had nothing to hide.

Here was this person doing what they wanted, no more and no less.

And to be that thing that she wanted? Well, then you'd stop performing like a fucking monkey.

And that's a peace few of us ever find.

Hmm?

And you could see all that in the assured grace of her arms.

And the way they moved.

And to be in those arms . . .

The next morning I packed a few things. I was going to London.

I left the house like I would any day. My boy was still in bed.

I'd heard him bring a girl in around four and I hadn't heard her leave.

My daughter was gone hours ago.

I wanted to see her before I went.

I was afraid I wasn't going to see her again.

I remembered when she was a little thing.

Crawling into bed beside me on a stormy night.

My hand up the back of her T-shirt. My hand wider than her back.

Her little feet on my knee.

My wife was out the back doing her flowers.

I watched her for a minute.

She was kneeling with a trowel.

She stopped and pushed her glasses up her nose with the back of her wrist. I didn't feel anything. I just left.

And nothing could have prepared me for the mad . . . fucking . . . things that were going to happen.

That's always the way. It's probably better.

I went to the bank, and then I went to the airport.

I was supposed to be reviewing some lunchtime shite in Bewley's.

And knowing I'd be up in the air by the time it went on, gave me a great, reckless . . .

I was doing something.

There wasn't a cloud in the sky. I was cradled up there.

I think I wanted it to crash.

But then the ground was solid, and this was real.

The air in London was heavy and still. I checked into a hotel and I went for a drink.

I wanted to find out where the cast were staying. Get Helen on her own. Be honest about it. Had to get busy doing this. Had to get busy, and I'll tell you why, because I didn't have a clue what the hell I was going to say to her.

I had a day before they arrived for rehearsals.

I did a little bit of relaxing.

Browsed in bookshops.

Sat in pubs. Walked around.

Down the Kings Road, across the Thames, into Battersea.
Not the best.

Took the bus back.

I saw the sights.

And I dumped my suit.

It was one I'd had for fifteen years.

Another quirk you see. I was full of that.

Had to get some natty duds. Impress the ladies. Changing
in a little cubicle.

Caught myself in the mirror.

Belly like a mountain. Little tits and everything. Suit hid it.
But the heat.

Got a linen jacket. And I went drinking.

And back at the hotel, in the early hours,

I took some hotel paper, hotel pen.

Coleridge on my shoulder.

Wrote a poem.

By the time I lay down, there was no paper left. It was all in
the bin.

And the big day dawned.

I had a dirty big fry and two pots of tea. Didn't feel like the
food of love.

I went down to the theatre, had a walk around.

I saw the scenery go in. And crates.

There was a pub across the road.

I had a quick couple of pints. Back out, walking around. No sign of the cast. Couple more pints.

Thinking about my editor and my wife. Wondering where I was. I'd had binges before. Not to worry, you know? It was that way. Be ringing each other. I never understood why she stayed.

What she saw in me. I couldn't see it.

The cast began to arrive in twos and threes up out of the tube.

But no Helen. She was another hour and a half. Arrived in a taxi. With Peter Hamilton.

What the fuck was this, you know?

She waited for him while he paid the fare. Then she linked his arm and they went inside. I went back in the pub and had a quick double, a bracer.

What were they doing together, you know? Maybe it was nothing.

A little fling at best.

Hamilton abusing his position. He was probably gay anyway.

And theatre people fuck like rabbits. Bucking each other up.

Didn't mean a thing. Nothing.

Compared to what I felt.

Another quick bracer.

At teatime they began to emerge. They were in good form. They were coming into the pub. I lashed out and bought a tweed hat. I pulled it down low and sat in a corner watching them over a newspaper.

Helen was surrounded by men.

It was so obvious. They kept touching her. It was hard to look at.

Finally Hamilton ordered them all to go home about ten.

They had a heavy day tomorrow.

This was it.

Helen left with Hamilton and two other actresses. I followed them.

We all took a tube to Victoria.

They were quiet. They were tired.

We changed trains. Main line.

Out into the suburbs. Out into Kent.

They got out near Bromley.

Went to a little terraced house.

I nipped into a shop, got a cheap bottle of scotch. Needed a bracer for this. I sat on the road and swigged for a little while. Maybe an hour.

And then, when I couldn't feel my heart anymore, I went to the house.

They must have been in bed.

Took a while to get an answer.

One of the other actresses, Cliona Leeson, opened the door.

She had a jacket on over her pajamas. She didn't recognize me with my hat. Peter Hamilton came down behind her, protecting the women.

I took off the hat and offered them the bottle. "Greetings," I said.

"Oh my God," said Hamilton. "What are you doing here?"

"Just a social call," I said. "And I'm looking for the chance to apologize for what my editor did to your review. He was at the show and he didn't agree with me at all."

Hamilton wasn't sure if this was a dream.

"He changed your review?" he said.

"I'm afraid so," I said. "He's always fancied himself. So, naturally, I've resigned from the paper, and here I am. Can I come in?" Hamilton didn't have a choice.

He wasn't the assertive type.

"Just for a minute," I said. "I realize it's very late."

Cliona Leeson yawned and went back upstairs. Left poor Hamilton to deal with this on his own.

He led me into a tiny sitting room, separated from the kitchen by a counter with stools, for playing at being out.

I made myself comfortable and Hamilton just stood smiling at me. Appalled.

He asked me if I'd like a cup of tea, but I was fine.

He gave me a glass for the scotch.

And I offered him a drink. He needed it. "I'll tell you, Peter," I said. "I've decided to come over to spread the word about the fantastic production you've done. The dogs in the street should beat down the doors to see it."

I was making as much noise as I could, you understand. I was waking the house. Helen would know I'd come for her. And I bellowed.

"What nobody seems to realize, Peter, is that you are probably the foremost director of your generation. But they're fools, aren't they? They're blind! They must be! You're the voice in the wilderness, aren't you?" I heard movement upstairs. Cliona Leeson was telling the others.

They were getting curious.

And I continued my tirade and tore into the bottle. I was even beginning to enjoy myself. But although Hamilton was stupid, he wasn't a complete idiot, and only a complete idiot could fail to see that his work was mediocre at best.

At fucking best, mediocre.

So much as he wanted to believe what I was saying, I was, in fact, making him very miserable.

But I couldn't give a fuck.

I was here to see Helen.

And sure enough, after a while, the girls had worked up their nerve.

There were footsteps on the stairs.

So they had a big day tomorrow. They had to work. But they were on tour, they were open to new experiences.

There may well be a story in all of this.

A famous theatre story.

The critic came to apologize.

Of course they'd come down. And down they came. Three shivering actresses.

Helen looked tired. She didn't look too good. And, when she looked at me, there was nothing,

And my resolve began to crumble, only slightly, but when I told them the review being changed story, I told it falteringly.

And I was running out of things to say about it. I had resigned on their behalf.

On behalf of a production that wouldn't even exist in two weeks.

It sounded like the lie it was.

But I was in for a penny now.

Hamilton wanted to believe me. I think.

It would do his career a world of good.

A critic resigning for his sake. He'd hang on to it.

Cliona Leeson seemed to be amused.

She was smirking into her cup.

Poor Helen looked too exhausted to care. But the third actress, Sheila Kilmeady, she was older. I knew her husband. He did a lot of television. I'd poured a pint over him about ten years before, at a time when I did that sort of thing because it got me the attention I wanted. And I'd brutalized him in the paper for a cameo he did in a British sitcom.

I'd said he was about as funny as wiping your hole with a Brillo pad.

God knows why I picked on him.

But we all need a purpose in life, even if we've got to make it up, ah?

And now, here was his wife, looking at me with all that sage wisdom culchies get when they move to the city and find out that saying smartarse crap for tourists isn't enough anymore. You have to work. And life is hard. And all that shit.

"You seem to have a problem with me taking a stand, Sheila," I said.

She looked at me for a moment and then she said, "I just don't believe you, that's all." And she went to bed.

Nobody said anything. It was all fucked now. Cliona Leeson and Helen followed her. Hamilton told me I was welcome to the couch. I thanked him and then I was on my own. And I realized how pissed I was. I knew I didn't want to be there in the morning. But. Helen. I'd . . . I'd . . . come to . . .

I'd come to say it.

Even if she was like them.

Even if she hated me. I'd come to say it. All I had to do was wait till they were asleep, talk to her on her own.

And maybe, why not? She'd pull back the covers and let me in and . . . Well. I don't know what. First things first. I had to wait.

So I sat there. And I drank. And I dropped off. I didn't dream. It was just black.

I felt something wet and I woke up.

I'd spilled the rest of the whiskey down my pants.

It was a quarter to six.

I stood up and I nearly fell over.

I went to the sink and I puked raw whiskey.

Burned the fucking throat off me.

I needed the toilet, I wasn't well.

It was a near thing getting up the stairs.

I just made it on to the jacks. I had the runs.

I leaned forward with my head in my hands.

And then I saw something.

It was jammed in behind the sink.

I pulled it out. It was a porno mag. Readers' wives. They were in bits. On their living room sofas, legs spread. Arses in the air.

And something lit in me I hadn't felt in a long time.

And I wanted Helen that way.

I wanted to hurt her.

I wanted her to feel it and beg me to stop and beg me to go on.

So I pulled up my pants and I checked the rooms.

It was bright now.

In one room. Hamilton and Cliona Leeson were in bed together. I could see her tits. It spurred me on.

Sheila Shitebag was in the next room with a pillow over her face.

All I had to do was exert a little pressure.

But I had things on my mind.

I pushed Helen's door open slowly.

Sunlight streamed across her bed. I've never seen anything like it.

I wanted to shag her.

All those years I'd sat in my study reading the Elizabethans. I'd forgotten what those poems were about. They were fore-play. They were all about having it off.

I knelt on the bed.

And I couldn't do it.

I couldn't move. Reason had crept into the room behind me and caressed my neck.

This girl. I could only crave her attention, and ruin her.

I was thinking about my girl you see?

I was thinking about something real.

I got up quietly and I left.

The traffic was beginning to thicken.

The first of the commuters.

I was walking west.

Canterbury was in Kent. Where Chaucer sent his pilgrims. Where Christopher Marlowe was born. He was murdered in Kent too.

Wasn't much of that now.

I walked the whole morning.

Had to keep taking a rest.

It was getting hot.

I went up into Crystal Palace Park. Through the long avenues of trees, up to the ruins of Crystal Palace itself. I lay there in the sun and I closed my eyes.

I'd made a total fool of myself.

I couldn't understand how I'd been so stupid as to think anything would have come of this. And I'd fucked myself up as far as Dublin was concerned. Everywhere I went people would laugh. I must have looked like a lunatic.

I was bollocks.

Chaucer's pilgrims went by.

Christopher Marlowe was arguing about the bill. My daughter climbed into bed beside me. And then someone pulled her out and I heard her screaming.

I woke up. It was dusk.

I was sweating booze.

I was thirsty. Miles from anywhere.

I had to get out of the park before it got too dark to see.

I scratched the gravel out of my hair stood up.

And as I did, I saw something move down by the steps. It was dark and huddled. I thought it was a big dog. I was frightened of dogs. I stood looking. I didn't want to provoke it by moving.

I was going to find another way out of the park. And then, suddenly, it stood up. It was a man.

He looked quite young. Thirty maybe. He started walking towards me.

For a second I thought I was going to be mugged, but there was something about him that made me comfortable.

It was relaxing to watch his easy stride. I just wanted to watch him walk.

As he got nearer I could see he was smiling.

"Beautiful night," he said.

"Yes," I said.

He stood beside me and we looked out over the lights of the city.

All those lives.

And then he said, "Getting dark. We'd want to get back to civilization."

"That's a good idea," I said.

And we began to stroll along.

It was like I'd known him for a long time.

It was natural for us to do this.

Down into the park. Very quiet.

"Were you asleep up there?" he asked me.

"I must have been," I said. "Rough night, last night."

He laughed and said, "I know what that's like."

Then he offered me his hand and said, "My name's William by the way."

We shook hands. He was cool.

Not cold, like you'd expect a vampire to be.

He was just right. I think I wanted him to touch my face. I wasn't sure. It was getting hard to think. It was easier just to walk.

(Interval.)

PART TWO

They have power. Not the power to make you do what they want.

But real power. To make you want what they want. It hurts to consider things in their company. It becomes hard to make sense. They appeal to the older part of us.

What we share with animals.

That's what they have you see.

So that when William hailed a taxi, I think I got in first.

I'm not sure how far we went.

We stopped on a wide suburban street. Old houses. Imposing pillars.

High trees.

I can still smell the house.

It was damp stones and running water and dry bark. It was familiar and exciting; I was sort of drifting you see.

The walls were paneled with dark wood. The carpets were a deep rich red.

An ornate banister.

We went into the kitchen.

It was warm and comfortable.

But there was something about it.

Took me a while to figure out what it was.

There was no food.

William put a bottle of Glenfiddich on the table and I took a good lash of it. He sat with me while I drank.

We didn't say anything.

It was quite dark, but I could see his eyes, bright, like a cat.

He seemed to be a bit embarrassed by it and he looked away.

I wanted to believe I was still dreaming.

I wanted to be afraid.

And then he said, "Six of us live here. The others are women. We need someone like you. It's better if we don't go out. We prefer it if people come here to socialize. Nobody dies, we only take what we need, and they don't become like us. We have always been like this.

"You can go to bars or clubs or wherever. Bring young people. There's a party here every night and you'll find they want to come with you. They leave unharmed and they never remember being here."

"Can you only come out at night?" I said. He smiled and said it was more convenient for them to live at night, because people are more willing to have a nice time then. "Is it a nice time?" I said.

He looked at me, his eyes pale, pale blue. "It's a wonderful time," he said.

And I believed him.

I was drunk. I was . . .

"Will you do it for me?" he said.

And I felt that saying no was like refusing a friend their dying wish. "Of course I will," I said.

And then I was very tired.

He brought me up the dark staircase to a door with more stairs and up into the attic. It was a low ceiling, a bed, a desk, a small window, a bathroom.

"You might like this," he said.

I turned and saw him standing at a bookcase. Everything I'd need.

I touched them. And I saw a bible. "You don't mind this book?" I said.

He shook his head.

"Nature made us both," he said. "And I don't like garlic because it makes my breath smell. That's the only reason.

"Superstition," he said.

Then he frowned and sat on the bed.

"I'll tell you something strange, though," he said.

"There's a tradition in Eastern Europe. You can keep a vampire away from your house by sprinkling rice on your windowsill. The vampire is compelled to count every grain, and luckily he'll still be counting when the morning comes. And for some reason that's sort of true."

I wasn't sure whether he was joking with me but he seemed to be serious.

He told me he had an overwhelming desire to know how many grains were in a pile. And he seemed to think there was something noble about that. Something that proved he had a deep sense of inquiry and not just a stupid obsession. Fucking rice . . .

That was the first sign I got of his vanity.

That he thought he was more than he was. He turned all his faults into virtues. But that night I was stupid enough and happy enough just to feel . . . ah!

He shook my hand and left the room. I sat at the desk and looked out at the tops of the trees.

And I found myself trying to miss my family. But something wouldn't let me.

I could only miss what they were like years ago.

And that's the way life is, you can't have that, can you?

You can't light a stranger's face with the mention of Santa.

You can only do that to certain people for a certain time.

And then nature makes everybody a cunt because one day you look around and you're all in each other's way.

Mm. There's always going to be a smugness about you listening to this.

As we all take part in this convention. And you will say, "These vampires are not very believable, are they?"

And you are entitled.

This convention. These restrictions, these rules, they give us that freedom.

I have the freedom to tell you this unhindered, while you can sit there assured that no one is going to get hurt. Possibly offended, but you'll live. We're all quite safe here. Safe to say things like, "If they were vampires, why don't their victims become vampires?" And you are, of course, relying on the lazy notions foisted upon you by others in the effort to make you buy more popcorn.

But when you find out that they are real, that all changes, you see.

Let's think about it, will we? For a moment. If a vampire bites you and you in turn become a vampire, that's a rule.

A causal, mechanical rule: "Vampirism is deadly contagious."

A rule that says their species, like ours, must survive. And that's natural, we suppose. And, that seems to make sense, fine. But we want it both ways.

We want the vampire's bite to be "magic." Death-defying, supernatural.

Why?

Why do we need it to be magic?

Because magic doesn't exist?

We don't have to be afraid of what doesn't exist.

Or is it because we envy them?

We're jealous of their power to instill fear in others.

And we can't have that, and if we can't, nothing can.

But we never seem to think for a moment that nature is magic.

We view nature scientifically. We can predict its laws.

But our pride in doing this blinds us. Blinds us to this simple fact: we don't know why there are laws at all.

We may know that the earth goes around the sun. And we may know that this is due to "gravity."

But not one of us knows why there is gravity. So don't sit there and cast judgment on the credibility of what I say, when you don't even know why you aren't floating off your seats.

I woke at the desk.

It was morning.

I could half remember hearing laughter during the night. Women.

It was another glorious day.

I had a wash and I went down.

The house was nowhere near as spooky in the bright. It was just dusty.

There was a note on the fridge. "This is for you." It was packed with food. There was food all over the place.

I went out the back. Sweet smell, rotten fruit.

I could just see the roofs of the houses on either side.

Just see them above the trees.

They needed repair.

And I knew no one lived there.

There were empty bottles all over the lawn and flies buzzed around the remains on the barbecue.

The sun was too much. I needed to be inside.

My wants were becoming very short term.

You see this was all part of it.

I spent the day reading up at my desk.

Drinking. A life of patronage. That's what I saw myself embarking upon.

Comfortable. I know.

Well.

I only noticed it was dusk when I heard movement downstairs.

Suddenly it was very cold.

There was a woman in the room.

She was black and her hair was dead straight.

She was sleek. Muscular.

I felt like I was floating backwards. That's the effect.

My spine melted into my belly and bubbled away there.

She held a bag out towards me.

I reached for it and she lightly scraped her nails over the back of my hand. And I was a baby wrapped up for the night. And then she was gone.

I sat there with my eyes half closed. Waves of well being rolling through me. The bag full of clothes. They were just the thing. Dashing. Disheveled and dashing. They were me.

I could hear more activity.

Doors banging. A row. Someone laughing.

And then footsteps on the stairs.

William.

"Good evening," he said. "You look good in that." Then he sat on the bed and said, "Mmm, days of cloistered reflection. Reading. Thinking. Are you ready to go?"

"Those women," I said.

"They won't bother you," he said, "they've been warned. Most beautiful women you'll ever see. But fall under their care, you'll wish you were dead, believe me."

Then he said I should get going.

"I don't know if I'm the social type," I said. He grinned at me.

"I think you'll find you are," he said.

He put some money on the desk and then he left.

I stood there, the light fading.

It was time to go. And . . . I suddenly felt . . . light on my feet. Energetic. I wanted to go out.

I went down. I didn't see anyone but it was like I could feel the anticipation. The house. The house had it.

Out on the road I was wondering which way to go, and a taxi just pulled up without me hailing it. I could feel that things were different. I was in it.

I was weak.

"Take me into town," I said.

That first night I did it.

I walked down into Leicester Square. The tourists and the ticket touts. How the living fuck I was going to invite anyone back to a party was quite fucking beyond me. As was why I was doing this. But Christ knows we all like to be busy. And. It's easy, when you're told what to do. When the choices narrow. When you're under authority. That's why there's so many madcap schemes and bad artists.

And why journalists wank so much, ah?

There's no excuse.

I went into a pub.

Everybody was standing.

I had a drink. I was looking around.

People finished work. Young people, with that shine off them.

This was ridiculous.

But then, suddenly, it wasn't the slightest bit ridiculous.

A young woman was at my elbow trying to get a round.

She was a blondy little thing with a pixie face.

"Excuse me," I said, and I moved sideways to let her get to the bar.

"Thanks," she said, "what'll you have? It's my birthday."

And I knew. I knew I'd been filled with charm. I'd been made attractive.

This was the gift I'd been given to bring people back.

"Your birthday!" I said. "Please, allow me."

"No," she said, "I couldn't, I'm with a group."

I looked around. They were perfect.

Twenties. Good looking. Lots of energy. "I'll have a pint, then," I said.

Her name was Dominique.

She worked for a magazine.

The people she was with were college friends. From Oxford.

She invited me to join them. Which I duly did.

And duly got bollocks out of my fucking face. And held them enthralled with my brutal wit. We looked like a bunch of saps and their rich daddy, I think. We were a tidy half dozen. At closing time we went for a pizza and wine, and more wine.

The stupid evening ablaze with drink and bullshit.

And then I had an "idea."

"Let's all go back to my house, for God's sake!" And I have to admit it. I was curious. I didn't like them. I was looking forward to seeing what was going to happen to them. I think you'd call that, having a streak in you.

And naturally by this time, we're inseparable and we pile into taxis.

All dry wit and our best clothes.

Chugging through the lights into the suburbs.

Down the dark road to William's house.

Music was drifting around from the back garden.

I led them down the side passage.

And I shut the gate.

There were candles lit all around the garden.

But there was no one there.

Tables were laid with drink.

We sat on stone benches.

I slugged on a bottle of wine.

But it was more than just being drunk in that place. It was like drowning. Gulping water for air and not being able to stop.

The youngsters fell around, dancing. In each others' arms.

And then, gradually, I noticed that there were more people. Moving among them.

The women. Jesus Christ. Heartbreakingly beautiful women.

You could see them and you couldn't.

Just like beauty in real life.

Sometimes it's there, and sometimes it should be. And it's not.

And after a while, I could feel the air. It began to fizz with pointless regret. And slowly, in twos and threes, they began to lie down in the grass.

And the moon and stars were shining down on this, and it was just another one of the things that goes on.

Nothing special.

I went to bed.

I woke up about ten.

Only the faintest twinge of a hangover. I'd gotten off lightly.

I went downstairs for some water, and there at the kitchen table, slumped over was Dominique.

I woke her. She was weak and she had a headache but that was all. I mean, fuck, I gave her some paracetamol, you know? I mean . . .

She couldn't remember anything about the party.

We went around waking her friends.

They were all over the place, on the floor, on the grass, one was even in a fucking hedge. I got them up.

Dominique gave me a kiss. I grabbed her hand. And they were happy, you know? They talked about getting a cure.

I saw them out. No harm done. I tidied up a bit. It was okay. Doing this. Being this thing.

I did it again the next night, and the one after. And after that. And that's how the next while was.

Flirting in bars. Getting . . . affection.

Back for a party. Getting them out in the morning. Everyone happy to be there and happy to leave.

Every time I did it, it was going to be the last time, but . . .

I'd think about the reception I'd get back in Dublin, and I wasn't up to it. I'd give it a few more days.

And . . . I'd keep giving it a few more days. I stayed away from the vampires, as much as I could.

The only one I spoke to was William. But I'd wish he'd leave me alone.

I'd be in the attic, and I'd read, and . . . I even began to do a little bit of writing. It was coming a bit easier, you see, because there were no knackers like me around the place who were going to tear it apart. It was just small things, things I'd remember. But I'll be straight with you. It wasn't very good.

And I'd be doing this you see and William would come to visit me.

I didn't want him to.

There was something.

He looked like us. But. He wasn't a human. And I had to think to work out what made him different.

And it was hard to think in that place. But I made the effort and I worked it out. How he was different from us. And it showed me what we are. What it is that makes us what we are.

But it took a good while.

I was curious about them of course. I began to have a look at them, sleeping. Sometimes they were all in the one bed. And sometimes I couldn't find them.

But they slept just like us.

And they'd wake up if I made a noise. Once, one of the women opened her eyes and I immediately got weak.

Weak in here. Took everything just to get back to my room.

And I had to lie down.

I stopped checking on them.

There was a gap.

And so, there I'd be, trying to write something. Trying to capture the care I once had, you see. My kids on Christmas eve. Something like that.

And I'd feel him come in.

And of all things, he'd talk about art. And advise me about writing.

It was always the same.

The art object is different from every other object, he said, because it's not for anything.

A chair only is what it is because it's for sitting on. A knife only is what it is because it's for cutting.

But art is for itself.

Just as goodness is. It's for it's own sake. Art is like having a go at making virtue. And he'd criticize me for my fear.

Fear of my work not being "good enough." The act itself is good, he said. You see how cerebral he was, nothing else. And I could never stand a pep talk. All that glib psycho-analytic wank.

So one day I got annoyed and said it must be brilliant, living for so long, gathering all this wisdom.

He didn't say anything for a while. He looked a bit shook. And then in his true, corny way, he told me a story.

A, Jesus, a fucking, story.

He told me there was a man where he came from, a long time ago.

And he was a woodsman.

And he was one of the happiest men who ever lived. Because he had married a woman who he loved more than himself.

His heart swelled at the thought of her. She was present to him at every moment of his lonely day out in the woods.

His only disappointment in life was that they couldn't have children.

Their innocence.

But it wasn't to be and he accepted his lot.

And that's what this man's life was like. And one day he was working out in the woods. And he heard someone crying. It was a strange sound. Near and far away at the same time. He dropped his ax and he went towards it. He called out and he was guided by the cries. And he saw why the sound was so strange. In the woods was a well and the crying came from the well.

He looked down, and in the water far below was an old man desperately clinging to the bucket, trying to stay afloat.

So the woodsman worked and strained and pulled him out. And then lay him down to recover. But it was too late. The old man was dying.

With his last breaths, he thanked the woodsman for his kindness and told him to look in his satchel. And in the satchel were tools for watchmaking. And there was a new watch.

The most beautiful watch the woodsman had ever seen.

The old man told the woodsman that he wanted him to keep it.

It could tell more than just the time he said. And then he died.

And it wasn't until many years later that the woodsman found out what the watch's secret was. He was out in the woods one winter's day and it was getting dark.

He looked at the watch but it had stopped.

He tried winding it but it didn't seem to work. But then he wound it backwards and something changed.

The light. Somehow it had become brighter. The sun was higher in the sky.

He wound it back another hour and the sun rose higher.

He could travel in time.

He wound it forward again and the sun went down.

Understandably he was a bit fucking amazed.

You see, this is the art of understatement. And he never told anyone about it, not even his beloved wife.

It was a secret.

And being an honest fellow, he never saw what practical use such a thing could have. He never used it to travel.

He wasn't interested. Everything he loved was in the present.

That was, until his wife died.

And the woodsman was heartbroken.

And naturally he couldn't resist going back a little, now and then, to hold her once again. And his infatuation never ceased.

He was fascinated by her.

He was in love, do you see?

And he began to go back a little further. Until it got to the stage where he went back further than he'd ever gone.

To see her as a child, before he had known her.

He was an old man watching this child play.

But this only made him feel his loss even more. He knew his time with her was over.

He faced up to it and decided he must live alone until he saw her again in heaven.

But he found that the watch was now truly broken and would not wind at all.

He was stuck in the past.

Where nobody knew him. Not even his wife, since she was just a little girl.

But she was all he had. He panicked.

Terror. He took the child.

He picked her up and ran into the woods with her in his frail arms.

And she was crying and screaming.

And he couldn't let her go.

And then he was tired and he couldn't go any further. And they fell together in the leaves. And he held on to her. You know?

And the townspeople caught him and beat him.

And left him.

When William finished telling me this we were . . . very quiet.

And then I asked him, what does it mean? And he didn't know.

He looked a bit bewildered. And then he laughed and fucked off.

He didn't know what his story meant.

He knew he was supposed to be informed by it but it was just a story that he told.

A story about not being able to get back.

And that was all.

And that's what makes us different.

We reflect.

They don't.

They see what they want. They get it.

Do anything to get it.

William couldn't hold a child anymore than, than you or I could push a glass of water away when we're parched.

And I think he wanted . . .

That was the horror of the whole thing.

The cunt wanted a conscience.

He fucking regretted not being able to regret the things he did.

And when I realized this, he began to disgust me.

Clinging to all this human bollocks, lecturing me on what was wrong with my life.

This unreflective animal. Christ.

All his foibles. His virtues. For fuck's sake. Man was a butcher. Slept all day.

Came out and bit people. Fucking knacker.

So it came to . . .

We were in the kitchen one evening before I went out for some youngsters.

And to be honest with you, as usual, I was a bit pissed.

There we were, leaning on the worktop, all philosophical. All ordinary.

How the world had fucked me up and this was where
I belonged.

Where there were no great expectations of me. Where
I could relax.

You know? Like he knew anything beyond how hungry he felt.

And this, the immorality of what I'd been doing over the
last few years.

Jesus, I knew that!

If I didn't I wouldn't have had a problem.

I knew what I'd been doing was wrong.

That's why I did it.

I enjoyed the looks of fear and hatred I'd gotten whenever
I went into an actors' pub.

I behaved that way, because it was wrong. But William had
no because.

He couldn't buck nature.

He had no choice the way a dog has no choice.

Reasons don't come into it.

And there he was talking to me about the autonomy of the
art object and things like this.

It was sad. It was boring.

And these vampire bitches moving through the house.
Brushing by.

These . . . things men would die for.

Getting in here. Bringing every whim you've got firmly down
into your pants.

I can't overstate their power to distract.

I was all confused whenever they came near me.

And William knew this. You know?

He'd let them be around, so I couldn't think straight.

So he could have the floor.

Fuck. He was welcome to it.

I had nothing to say to him.

I just thought, Ah, Jesus, would you just . . .

You know?

And I grabbed this jar of rice and I smashed it on the floor.

William was a bit startled at first, but then, suddenly, I was just another object in the room. And him, and I think two others . . . got down on the floor and started to count. I thought I better get going.

William was saying, Wait, come, come back.

But he was lost in the rice.

And I had a moment of clarity.

No more messing . . .

This was the last night I was doing this. This was the last batch of idiots I was bringing back.

And after that . . . Well I didn't know. I'd see.

I took a cab into Soho.

A bar with a late licence.

I sat there for a few hours and it began to fill up as all the other bars closed.

It was a kip, and I had to be the oldest codger in the place.

But the old charm was there and pretty soon I was getting greeted. And smiled at. Who did they think I was, for fuck's sake? And I was at the bar with this group of rich kids.

Exchanging stories about the old days that are all gone now.

Oh yeah, I knew them all. Name them. I knew them. He was a drinker. Let me tell you. Let me tell you. Mmm.

What are we doing here? I know somewhere we can go. Yeah.

I think I was aware of her before I saw her.

The first thing I saw was her feet.

Bare feet in open sandals.

The sinews in her ankle shifting with her weight.

Helen.

She was looking at me.

These people were actors.

She had every right to stare at me.

What I'd done.

And as far as anyone knew, from Dublin, I had disappeared.

And here I was regaling the young things in London.

I looked her in the eye.

I could feel the tears coming.

Made me annoyed.

I was embarrassed.

I wanted to kill everybody. Get out.

But I'd forgotten the charm, hadn't I?

She leaned forward and kissed me.

I could have anything I wanted.

"People have been wondering about you," she said.

"People . . . Let me get you a drink," I said. And I bought a round.

You see this was the first time I'd been surrounded by artists and actually felt in charge.

This was the ideal last batch.

In the morning, none of them would remember what had happened.

And I would know.

And they'd be fools in my eyes forever. I had power now.

But Helen.

This could be different in her case. In our case.

I could keep her away from the others.

Bring her up to the attic. Lock the door.

And she'd be . . .

She'd want to lie down with me.

Until it got bright.

And a big clock would go back, and when we woke up, how the world would have changed. That was my wish.

"Let's go," I said.

"Come on." And we piled into cabs. And for the second time in as many months she was beside me.

Her cool body.

A soothing fucking you know? A . . .

And all the others were drunk as maniacs.

I leaned into her.

"You've got to stay beside me tonight," I said. She didn't even question it. I was beginning to miss things.

The spell was breaking.

Human company.

We got to the house.

Probably the most people I'd ever brought back.

I held her hand.

And I led everybody around the back.

And I got a shock.

The vampires were there already.

All around the garden.

Quiet. Watching us. No music tonight. The young actors didn't care.

They were caught up in the easy confusion of the place. Ten times as drunk as when they'd left the bar.

And the worst thing.

William was only looking at me.

He was annoyed at me.

I'd let him down.

He'd been all clever one minute and the next he was down on the floor counting rice.

I'd reminded him what he was and what he wasn't.

The women didn't waste any time.

Already there were tangles of limbs.

And William was just looking at me.

I took Helen into the house.

She was nodding off.

I had to get her out.

I began to panic.

As much as one can panic when every thought is like looking for something in . . . tar. We went into the hall.

And one of the women was on the stairs.

I couldn't move.

I couldn't feel Helen.

She was gone.

The woman came towards me.

I was in for it.

My legs began to wobble.

She took me in her arms and lifted me. Dancing slowly in the hall.

We were up the banister, we were down in a corner. We were drifting.

The joy of submitting to something like that.

To put yourself in someone's care.

Trust has nothing to do with it.

It's abandon.

And then the stupid cow bit me.

And it fucking hurt.

My arm was getting cold.

I passed out.

And then, thump, we were on the ground. I could feel my weight again.

I was a fat bastard on the floor.

The woman was on top of me.

She was dozy.

There was blood all down my shirt. Down my pants.

Only consolation I had was she might get a hangover that'd knock her off her feet for days. She'd bitten the wrong fellow. It would have been nice to lie there for a while. But the alarm bells were ringing. I had to find Helen.

Fuck. I couldn't believe I'd been bitten. I went back out to the garden.

Dawn was coming. The vampires were gone in. People lay about.

Helen wasn't there.

She wasn't in the kitchen or the lounge. She wasn't on the stairs.

Then I heard talking.

It was in the attic.

It was William.

His singsong.

His lilt.

I crept up. Slowly.

He was talking about me.

About the world and how it had spoiled me.

Ah, he was spoofing.

Pretending he could think.

I got to the door.

Helen was on my bed.

She had hardly any clothes on.

She'd been bitten too.

And William was sitting beside her.

Talking rubbish.

The epitome of nature's thoughtlessness.

The desire to survive.

That's all he was.

But he didn't know that.

And looking at the two of them there. No comparison.

She was so beautiful.

And he was a black-looking thing that was hardly even there.

And I was more her than him. A good feeling.

And I just said, "Leave her alone, you smelly prick."

He looked up at me, and I swear to God, his eyes were
blazing red. I'm not joking. But, because of that, the situa-

tion didn't seem very real. And I wasn't scared. "Helen," I said, "get up."

She obeyed me the way a sick child does.

Slowly, with resignation.

"Do you want me to leave?" he said. "No, stay there," I said, "I'm going."

He looked at the bookcase for a moment, and then he said, "You won't be happy."

"Probably not," I said. "But it wouldn't be much fun if I was." Know what I mean?

Then I put my arm around Helen and brought her down the stairs.

He didn't follow us and I don't know why he let me go.

Maybe wanting a conscience is the same as having one.

Because it's all the same effort, isn't it? Maybe he was just imitating us.

I lay Helen on a couch with one of her pals. She slept. I gave her a kiss, and then I left them to their hangovers.

The summer was fading.

There was a chill in the morning.

I walked down the street and I thought about the fuss people were going to make of me.

The potential it gave me to bully sympathy out of everybody.

Back from my breakdown.

On the right track again, yeah?

I'd "Embrace My Second Chance."

I'd do a piece about "Getting Back."

Getting back in touch with things.

Talking To My Wife.

Giving My Children My Advice.

I had my health.

I had resolve.

But most important.

Over everything else.

I had a story.

So, were they real?

Or were they a dream?

Well, I've got to ask you, what the hell isn't a dream?

Your projections for the future. Your fantasies.

Your fears. Your rude awakenings.

What the hell is that, if it's not any night's sleep?

And that person you fell head over heels for.

What the hell was that?

What was the moment it hit you?

Love, Christ. If it was love at first sight, what the hell you doing giving some stranger the benefit of the doubt? Entrusting them with everything you've got?

Because of what you wanted them to be?

Well, that's a dream-life if ever there was one.

And if it wasn't love at first sight, and it was a gradual thing. Like a wound healing.

Let me ask you this: don't you begin to resent that person in equal amounts? For sneaking up on you, and denying you all the chaotic excitement you felt your love should have been?

And if neither of these are true for you and you're in the middle of it, and you haven't fucking blown it yet. And you're the happiest person in the room . . .

Well, your presence blesses everyone else here, doesn't it? Because you're the embodiment of hope, aren't you? You're hope incarnate.

Where are you? Where are you?

Where?

End of Play

THIS
LIME TREE
BOWER

For Jack McPherson and Rionach

A delight
Comes sudden on my heart, and I am glad
As I myself were there! Nor in this bower,
This little lime tree bower, have I not marked
Much that has soothed me.
. . . No sound is dissonant which tells of life.

SAMUEL TAYLOR COLERIDGE
"This Lime Tree Bower My Prison"
1797

PRODUCTION HISTORY

This Lime Tree Bower was first performed at the Crypt Arts Centre, Dublin, on September 26, 1995. It was an Íomhá Ildánach/Fly by Night coproduction. The lighting was by Paul Winters, the design was by John O'Brien and Conor McPherson. It was produced by Philip Gray and directed by Conor McPherson. The cast was:

JOE	Ian Cregg
RAY	Conor Mullen
FRANK	Niall Shanahan

The play was subsequently performed with the same cast at the Bush Theatre, London, on July 3, 1996. The lighting was by Paul Russell and Conor McPherson was the director.

CHARACTERS

JOE, seventeen

RAY, early thirties

FRANK, twenties

All remain on stage throughout,
and are certainly aware of each other.

JOE

Damien came to our school halfway through the term.

He was different from everybody else there.

Even his uniform made him look good.

He had a long fringe, bleached, and he had a tan.

He always smoked and he never went home at lunchtime.
I found out that he didn't live too far away, and he probably
had the coolest bike in the whole school, but at lunchtime,
he hung around.

I started smoking too, so I could talk to him at little break
behind the religion room. It was completely fucking disgusting.

You were supposed to be dying for a pull and about nine
blokes would be sharing a fag. By the time it came around to
you it was just a soaking wet filter.

And you had to drag on it like you'd die without it.

But I got to talk to Damien.

I pretended my bike was broken and I brought sandwiches in so I could hang around at big break.

The lads who stayed in all got chips in the Chinese, which I wouldn't get because of what my dad had told me about them.

The lads who ate them all had huge spots, except for Damien.

He was only in three of my classes, and one of them was civics, which we only had once a week, but I could never wait for him to come in.

He was never on time and in the mornings if I was in a room where I could see the driveway, I'd watch for him.

I never once saw him arrive but he'd always be there.

That's the way it is when you like someone—you can never see them.

I tried to tell Frank, my brother, about Damien, but he called me a poofter and told me to go asleep.

Frank was five years older than me and worked with my dad in our chipper.

I only worked there during the holidays.

It was never busy till then.

No one comes to the seaside when it's raining, which is weird, because that's when I liked it best.

When it was all gray and the waves splashed up on the road is when I liked it.

Those sort of days my dad had a pint in Reynolds and read the paper.

I used to go in and sit with him sometimes.

Like on a Saturday.

He told me once that drinking is no way for a man to sort anything out, but that he only found out too late.

I told him not to be silly.

Frank said that Dad's problems were none of his doing.

He owed a big loan to Simple Simon McCurdie.

Simple Simon was a councillor and owned the bookies down the street.

Frank said he was far from simple.

We didn't know how he got the name.

But he had it.

And that's what we called him.

I'm quite shrewd and I know how to do things in ways that don't look really obvious.

That's how I made friends with Damien.

We'd just find ourselves standing together.

I saw what bands he had, written on his bag and on his journal.

I let on to like them too.

And because he'd come halfway through the term, he didn't know anyone.

Sometimes I'd pretend not to see him and he'd still come over to me.

So I knew he liked me.

He was kicked out of his last school for being on the mitch and smoking in P.E.

He had told a teacher to fuck off and she had just got out of hospital or something and she started crying.

He was lucky to get into our school because not many places would take someone like that.

But then, my school was a dump.

Someone who lived near Damien said he hadn't been expelled at all.

He had left because he was always being slagged for only having one ball.

But somebody always says something.

I reckon our school had pity on him because he needed somewhere to do his leaving.

He told me about the girls he'd shagged and how he could always tell when someone was a virgin.

I blushed so badly that I had to pretend to blow my nose so he wouldn't see.

He asked me to bonk off school one Friday.

I'd never done it before and I knew I'd be killed.

But Damien said he was an expert forger and he'd give me a brilliant note.

We arranged to meet at the roundabout on the dual carriageway at nine o' clock.

I was waiting for ages.

I thought everyone was looking at me.

And I knew that Miss Brosnan, our biology teacher, used to drive around looking for boys on the mitch when she had a free class. She had huge tits and we used to pretend there was something wrong with the microscopes so she'd bend over to have a look.

I was imagining her catching me on the mitch and making me fuck her as a punishment.

I was too scared to go off on my own and I was going to go in late and get detention.

But then Damien showed up.

He didn't even have his uniform on.

We cycled around the suburbs and stayed off the main roads. It felt brilliant.

All the people were at work.

I saw women wheeling kids out of the supermarket and I thought about me being with my mum when I was like that.

We went into the park.

It was dark under the trees and we scrambled up and down the hills.

Then it was nearly one and we sat down and ate our lunch.

We could see two girls from Holy Faith going through the park to the shops.

Damien knew them.

They were gorgeous and I felt like an ugly bollocks.

One was blond and one was dark like she was foreign.

Damien made them laugh about people they knew and I didn't.

I wanted to hold their hands and stroll through town with lots of money.

They didn't say anything to me, but they looked at me like if I was with Damien, there must be something good about me.

But they couldn't see what.

I sucked in my cheeks and pretended not to be interested.

I fiddled with my gears and broke them.

When the girls were gone we sat under the trees where we could see the beach.

My stomach was all tingly.

Damien said the blond one, Tara, would ride anybody. She had had it off with most of his friends and Damien had screwed her when he was fourteen.

I asked him how it had happened and I immediately felt like a cretin.

Damien just said, "Got a boner. Stuck it in."

Then he went off for a piss and he was gone for ages.

I had to go looking for him, but when I found him I let on I was just cycling around.

He told me his dad was living with some woman and that his mum had had him when she was sixteen.

He started saying how cool she was and we should go home and see her.

I told him school wasn't over yet.

He said his mum couldn't give two shits.

They lived out by the Old Strand Road where all the Protestants lived.

The house had a long front garden with high trees. There was a boat in the drive but Damien said it didn't go.

There was a lawnmower in the hall and the carpet was filthy.

There was a spicy smell.

We had toast and peanut butter and watched MTV. There were bottles everywhere.

I looked out the back. The garden was lower than the front.

Then Damien's mum came in.

She was small and she had jeans and runners.

She didn't look like any of the mums I knew.

She had too much makeup and I could see she had no bra.

She ignored me and asked Damien why he wasn't in school.

A man came in behind her and went straight out the back.

A huge dog ran after him and the man took off his shirt.

I watched him run around with the dog and then he jumped into a muddy pond at the bottom of the garden, with his pants still on.

Damien shouted at his mum not to give him a hard time—
she was doing his head in.

She stopped giving out then and gave him a kiss.

He put his hand on her arse and she was looking at me and
giggling.

I was sort of laughing too, but I didn't think it was funny.

I was being false.

I went out pretending I really had a thing for dogs. The dog
didn't come near me though. I sat in the kitchen door and
watched the man.

He was putting his head under the water and coming up
saying, "Jeeesus, Jeeesus Christ!"

Damien came out and I asked him who the man was. But
Damien didn't know. He must've been a friend of his mum's
he thought.

The man shouted at us not to mind him because he was a
bit pissed.

Damien's mum came out and said, "Peter, What are you
doing?"

Then she laughed and ran down to the pond.

I went home then.

Damien wanted me to stay but I felt funny.

Then I was too early.

I had to wait outside Simple Simon's bookies for a quarter
of an hour till school was over.

Simple Simon saw me and came out.

He was really fat and he scared the shit out of me.

He leaned against the door frame all chummy with his arms
folded.

He didn't say anything for a minute, like we were really used to each other.

Then he asked how Dad was.

I said alright, thanks.

"Good, good," he said.

He was always saying that, "Good, good," like it was some catchphrase the audience loved.

Then he showed what a bollocks he was and asked me if I was on the mitch.

I said no.

And he said, "Why are you hanging around here then? What are you waiting for?"

He said it like he was going to slap me but then he broke his shit laughing.

I gave him the false laugh I was getting good at and cycled off.

He told me to say hello to Frank for him.

Frank said Simple Simon was a fucking leech when I told him.

He was wiping tables and filling ketchup in our sit-down part.

Dad was out the back with his head under the bonnet. He asked me how school was.

I shouted fine and ran upstairs.

I lay in my room and wanked and thought about the girls in the park, and they loved me because there had been a nuclear blast and there was no one left in the world.

Only us. They had to share me.

They had to take turns.

It was just to have a good wank.

Because the girl I really fancied was Deborah Something.

She lived down the road and I'd only ever seen her from the side.

My sister Carmel was in the shower because her boyfriend Ray was coming.

He had a great car because he had this really good job lecturing in a college.

He gave out about it a lot.

He said the thickest people he ever met were all in third-level institutions.

One time he showed us a journal called *Ethics* because he had an article in it.

I couldn't grasp what it was about but you could see he was clever.

Him and Dad and Frank would sit up drinking whiskey and watching the late news programs. Then they'd give out about the politicians and the reporters and anybody they saw.

They slagged what everybody said and the way everybody looked.

That was the way it was.

I don't know what Ray was doing hanging around with my sister.

Maybe he wasn't clever all the time.

Or just blind.

RAY

I woke up on a cold October morning in bed with one of my students.

What was her name? I can't remember.

I got up, put on my Dunnes Stores' jumper and underpants.

I always wore khaki trousers in those days.

It was kind of . . . a thing with me.

The room was freezing.

All the usual shit. Paper lightshade, Stone Roses poster,
a load of fucking awful books I'd never read and all the
empty bottles of wine she'd drunk over the last God knows.

Her hair was sticking out over the quilt.

She was a bit of a chubby yoke, and for a minute I felt like
hopping back in and giving her one. From behind.

But it was a passing yen and I had a lecture to give at twelve.

I felt like absolute shite.

I was putting on weight and I needed a haircut and a shave.

Had to wash my face in cold water.

Didn't bother waking her up. Fuck her.

I went down and got into the Saab.

And just my luck, it was always a bitch to start on a cold
morning.

By the time I got it going she was looking out the window.

I pretended not to see.

She turned away quickly and I just knew she was going to
leg it down to the garden. But by that time I was long gone.

Going down the dual carriageway, me, Pat, Elaine and the
fucking Morning Crew, and my hangover was coming into
its own.

I'd started the afternoon before with a quiet pint in the student bar.

Now I always drank in the student bar because I hate academics.

I don't really like students either, but there you are.

Well a few of them joined me and they're buying me pints.

And what do you know? It's nine o'clock and there's a disco on.

Girl from my third-year utilitarianism group in a leather mini and I'm up dancing.

One of the kids . . .

And I was thinking about these sort of German Bohemians in Hamburg trying to understand the Beatles. Like these kids trying to work me out. See what makes me tick.

We paused for cocktails. There was a tequila promotion on. Few of them and I'm back up again.

For a minute, I forgot who I was.

And then I remembered and I spun 'round and 'round like a kid and it was all coming back and then I puked right there in front of everybody.

People slipped in it, the place was mayhem.

The lights came on and for some reason I offered to pay for the mess.

Then it was time for lifts home.

Out into the wind and drizzle.

There's five of them in the fucking car.

I was annoyed now.

Someone put on a tape. It was a comedy thing which wasn't remotely fucking funny.

First stop, Blackrock. Two girls get out.

They're talking philosophy in the back of the car. This fucking kid with long manky hair is nearly screaming some stupid theory about Karl Popper so I'll hear him and . . . remember him forever, or give him a job or something.

And everyone else is going, "Just shut the fuck up, Vyvyan." Back across the dualer into Goatstown.

Then it's just me and her.

She lives in Mount Merrion.

She invites me in.

I check she doesn't live with her parents—happened to me before when I was working as a tutor in England.

I was banging this first-year in the morning and her mother came in to wake her for college. You can't take anything for granted.

It was cool. So in we go. I crash on her bed. I wake up. Three in the morning. I roll over. We do it.

It was shite.

Anyway, into college.

I parked behind the bar and thought about how long it had been since I was in there. Eleven and a half. Eleven and a fucking half hours.

I had to give a twelve o' clock in Theatre O. I'd enough time to get a cure.

I sat in the filthy bar and laid into about four gin and tonics because I'd heard somewhere that they were supposed to be good for a hangover.

But that's probably bullshit too.

Nothing works except getting pissed again.

It's a dreadful fucking world, isn't it?

I made up my mind not to feel guilty.

Carmel could never find out. Our lives were too separate.

Of course, this was something I could lose my job over. But it was just the state I was in I couldn't give a fuck.

I waffled my way through the lecture.

There were only about twenty there.

The rest probably all had hangovers.

I fucking turned up. Ingrates.

Up in my office the wind was howling.

I watched the trees blowing.

I went and had a huge shite.

Then I put my head on my desk and snoozed.

I dreamt I'd organized a recording of *Under Milk Wood* in my flat.

John Rawls came down from the mountains and his wife was choosy about what she ate.

I woke with someone knocking at the door. I looked at my watch.

Three o'clock. Twelve hours since I'd rolled over.

And there she was at the door.

She came in and started crying.

I gave her a tissue. Told her it wasn't a big deal.

I joked with her and she cheered up.

With some girls it's just about pushing the right buttons, isn't it?

We drove to a quiet pub out near Rathfarnham.

After a few drinks and something to eat, I said, "Friends again?" She smiled.

Yeah, we'd been stupid. We admitted it.

But we were adults.

We could put it behind us.

There was nothing to worry about.

Inside, I was seething.

Thinking about what a stupid fat bitch she was. Doing this on me.

Her little moment of glory.

I couldn't breathe. My stomach was full of acid.

I nearly lost my temper but I kept my cool.

At seven I gave her a lift into town.

She was going to the Stag's Head.

All I needed now was for her to have a bun in the oven.
That'd be just fucking great.

It was time to see Carmel.

Carmel had these . . . country virtues.

That whole Greek idea of the good life.

The life lived well.

I fancied a few beers with her brother, Frank. Shoot the shit
for a while and then later, when everyone was in bed me and
Carmel would go up to her room.

You see, I was sort of in the middle of an experiment in
those days.

I wanted to have a really vigorous fuck and break the condom.

Driving down the Malahide Road, I touched ninety twice.

Life in the old girl yet.

FRANK

I remember that Friday.

The weather had been rotten all week.

It was freezing when I woke up.

Dad was out the back, messing with the car. I told him to
leave it and let Ray have a look. Ray knew a few bits and
pieces about engines and that. He was a great driver. And he
usually called over to see Carmel on a Friday.

Dad was always fucking around with the engine. It was an old Peugeot 205.

He never went anywhere in it since Mum died. He didn't have the will.

He didn't have any reason to go in it.

And this made him think there was something wrong with it.

People always blame something, don't they?

I normally got up about eleven.

We opened at twelve on the dot.

I had just sort of drifted into working with Dad. He couldn't afford to pay me a fortune.

But I was living at home.

I had no overheads.

It was boring but it was better than nothing.

Because there's nothing worse than a seaside town in the winter when there's nobody about.

We had our regulars at lunchtime.

They'd come around from the bank and the shopping center.

That was a little belt for about an hour.

Then about four, people would send their kids in for the tea.

Friday teatime was always good.

Sevenish, it'd slack off till the pubs closed.

We stayed open till one at the weekends, half eleven, twelve on weekdays.

It was usually just me and Dad.

But sometimes Joe would drag his heels around, "working."

But he hated it.

Carmel was too busy to help.

She was being trained as something at the new financial services center in the city, which sounded good. But she never said much about it, so it was probably a load of shite.

I had a couple of nights off, midweek, when Dad just did take-aways.

There was nothing to do, except sit in Reynolds bar and listen to the old lads going on about when the INLA split from the officials and all that sort of thing they could get into a fight about.

If Simple Simon McCurdie was there, they'd use him as a sort of umpire.

He'd sit at the bar with a bottle of Blackbush and nod at them wisely whenever anyone mentioned Seamus Costello or Cathal Goulding.

I'd head back to give Dad a hand about eleven.

First thing in the morning, I'd turn on the fat and the telly.

Anne and Nick were my favorite—Nick always seemed to be taking the piss out of Anne. I'd have it on in the back and just be listening to it while I worked.

I did the chopping and cleaning while Dad did the batter.

He'd lost a lot of weight over the last while and he was drinking too much but he was cheerful and everybody liked him.

Since I'd been sort of full-time we'd been getting on great.

He had all these stories he kept telling over and over with little exaggerations getting worse all the time. But I never got tired of them.

Just before twelve, he'd have his first small one of the day.

He said it helped his blood flow more easily.

I'd gotten used to it, but sometimes I felt it was a bit early.

Because he'd have a couple with his dinner, and from teatime on, he'd sort of be topping it up.

That Friday I opened up a bit late.

People came in from about half.

I took orders in our sit-down part and Dad would put them on the counter.

I was like a waiter and the people knew me. I'd chat with them. Have a laugh.

Mostly though, people took their food away.

Then, about two, Simple Simon came in with his nephew, Charlie Dunne.

I was pissed off because they went into the sit-down part.

Dad wiped his hands and told me to get behind the counter. And he went to deal with Simple Simon himself.

Simon was a local councillor and had the only bookies in the town.

Dad owed him a couple of grand.

He borrowed it when Mum died.

He should've gone to a bank or the credit union, but he'd owed Simple Simon money before from stupid bets.

And Simon used to let him off.

He knew Dad wasn't going anywhere and if it came down to it, Dad could always give him a share in the chipper.

So Dad, like a fucking gobshite, thought he had a special relationship.

As if friends could never let money upset them.

Well he was learning the hard way because now Simon was calling in the loan.

And it was killing my dad.

I knew one of the reasons he kept tinkering with the car was because he was wondering if anyone would buy it.

But it could only go for parts and he'd be lucky to get two hundred for it. Like very lucky.

And I hated Simple Simon because he knew exactly what he was doing.

It would break your heart to see Dad trying to butter him up and Simon playing the patient generous old uncle.

He was a miserable cunt.

He wanted a smoked cod and chips and his nephew Charlie wanted a quarter pounder with cheese, two battered sausages, chips and bread and butter.

Simple Simon used to always introduce Charlie as "my sister's boy."

"This is Charlie, my sister's boy," he used to say. I think he said it to reassure people that Charlie wasn't some sort of scientific experiment.

His head was too big but his face was tiny.

And his arms were too long so he always had his hands in his trouser pockets like he couldn't stop playing with himself.

I wanted to spit in their tea but Dad would've killed me.

When I brought their stuff over Simon was acting like me and him shared some big secret that we both found funny.

He was always offering me a job.

He told me his fingers were in lots of pies and there were fewer and fewer ways out of this town.

I pretended I'd love to take him up but told him that my dad needed me.

He told me to think about it and he squeezed my elbow.

Charlie asked me for "Red Sauce," which the rest of us know as ketchup and it gave me an excuse to fuck off.

They stayed for ages.

Simon read *The Independent.*

And Charlie didn't do anything.

He just sat there with his hands in his pockets.

And he seemed perfectly fucking content just to do that.

It scared the shit out of me.

It must have been getting on for three when they left.

Dad ran out after them to say good-bye, wiping his hands like Simple Simon was going to check them.

Charlie nodded at me. I was fascinated by the size of his head so I nodded back.

To make him do it again.

Of course, they didn't pay and my dad shot me a look that said he didn't want to hear any shit from me.

And I think it was then that the mad plan started to form.

And once it started, I couldn't stop.

There was a big bloke with a beard used to come into Reynolds the odd time.

The old lads always bought him drinks, but he wouldn't chat much.

Most people steered clear of him.

He'd only ever come in the chipper about nine, when it was quiet. And he was usually there on a Friday.

If it was me serving him, I'd have a cup of tea while he ate. We'd talk shit mostly, and I wouldn't say I knew him partic-ularly well. But I had heard a few different stories about him, in Reynolds.

Fran Ferris said he was a gunman from the North who'd escaped and they couldn't extradite him. Shamey Devereaux said he was an armed robber out on parole trying to stay out of trouble.

This could well have been a load of bollocks and he might have worked in Super Value—but I have to admit, there was something about him. And as far as I knew, Reynolds was the only place would even serve him.

That night, Ray called about eight and he was upstairs with Carmel and Dad.

Joe was in our room and it was a fairly safe bet he was having a wank.

Everyone thought he was great.

He was always studying.

The bloke with the beard came in about half nine.

He asked me for a fresh cod and chips.

I was wondering what type of person he was.

The only thing I definitely knew about him was that he liked fish.

He was reading his paper when I brought it over to him.

The place was empty.

My heart was banging away like the Peugeot.

I sat down opposite him.

"Listen," I said, "I may be barking up the wrong tree completely, but I want to ask you something."

He kept on eating and didn't look at me.

"What is it?" he said.

"I need a gun."

He took a sup of tea and then he put it down and said, "What do you want it for?"

I ate one of his chips.

JOE

I spent the evening with Fergus and Noel.

We were mates since being kids.

They called for me and we had nowhere to go.

We went down to the rocks where the shipwreck was. The tide was out and we could see most of it.

We were never allowed to swim out near it because a boy got stuck in it one time and died. But that was back in the seventies and none of us knew him.

The story was that the ship was carrying guns for the IRA in 1920 or something and the captain was an English fellow who had fallen in love with a girl in the town.

And she was in the womens' IRA.

And she got him to bring the guns over in the night. But she was supposed to marry some farmer further up the coast. And he had found out and and he tipped off the Black and Tans. So they arrested the girl in her house and captured the IRA men who were going down the beach to get the guns.

But the girl knocked over an oil lamp in the house and there was a huge fire.

This warned the captain of the boat and he scuttled it.

He was drowned and because a British soldier died in the fire the girl was hung.

That was the story the old lads in Reynolds used to say about it.

But Frank told me the boat belonged to a fisherman called Vinty Duggan who crashed it after drinking a bottle of Powers.

It was hard to know who to believe.

The town was full of spoofers.

Dad said he wouldn't get involved in the dispute because he was from Italy and it was none of his business.

He said that Irish people would rather make something up and if that's what they liked to do, then he had no problem.

When I told him he was forgetting I was Irish, he just told me to believe what I liked.

Or better still, make up my own spoof about the boat.

But I wasn't really bothered. I just liked looking at it. Lots of things could have been true, who knows?

Fergus and Noel were skulling rocks at the boat and I was having a piss in the sea and I saw the girl I fancied, Deborah Something, up on the promenade.

She was walking along with some bloke.

I felt shit.

We went down to the amusements.

There was only one game I really liked.

It was an old one with a big rifle and you shot at targets that went back into the distance. Even though they were just a few feet away. They just got smaller.

It was only 10p still, because no one ever played it.

When I got home the chipper was closed.

Frank and Carmel and Ray and Dad were watching some film with lawyers and rain.

But only Carmel was really watching it.

The men were drinking and chatting.

I said good night and had a shower.

There were clean sheets on my bed and on Frank's. I looked at Frank's books.

He had lots of thrillers and westerns.

I liked his books because the sentences were always short.

The writers gave you the facts.

In school we did books where nobody said what they meant and you had to work out what everybody wanted.

I picked out a book with a black and silver cover.

I always read what the newspapers had said about the book.

Things like, "You won't find better pace anywhere," *Chicago Tribune*.

Or, "I couldn't put it down. The quickfire dialogue and action set-pieces make this a winner," *Los Angeles Times*.

These books knew how to be read.

They usually started with somebody looking at their watch.

"Jack Brannigan looked at his watch and quietly cursed . . ." That type of thing.

They also had good sex bits.

Girls whose nipples went as hard as peach stones and their soft skin became covered in goosebumps.

The blokes all had big mickeys and they came quickly the first time.

The next was slow and leisurely.

I read fifty pages of this book.

The ex-cop was a drunk, but he was trying to stay sober.

He was looking for the daughter of a drug dealer who'd been kidnapped.

He knew the city.

But it was changing.

It was summer.

I went under the covers and curled up in the clean sheets.

I was an ex-cop. But I had good in me.

Justice. That kid I shot was an accident.

I woke up when Frank came in.

He was chuckling. I could smell the drink.

I liked Frank, I wanted to be like him.

"Hey Frank," I said.

"What's the story, Joe?" he asked me.

He was always asking me what the story was. It was three in the morning.

I asked him if he was going to bed.

He just kept laughing.

He told me to go asleep. But I turned on the light. I wouldn't leave him alone till I knew what he was laughing at.

He told me he was going to hold up Simple Simon's bookies.

I asked him when. He said Monday.

And I just thought he was really pissed.

I lay down and I thought about Damien.

I wished it was Monday so I could see him.

I wanted to talk to him about something we were both interested in.

But I couldn't think what that was.

RAY

During the weekend, I drove around with Carmel. The weather picked up and we played tapes. That sort of thing.

I sometimes felt a bit guilty.

Carmel beside me in a light print dress and my mind wandering into different beds.

We stopped for lunch in Longford.

I watched Carmel talking.

She was intelligent.

Probably even more intelligent than me.

But I was together and worldly and she was innocent and trusting.

She had that nobility some people have about them. This showed me what I was and I thought it was a good thing our souls don't have smells.

Because mine would stink.

But at the same time I was proud.

I was getting away with it.

We decided to keep going for Galway and spend the night.

I liked it when a Galway station came on the radio. It was like coming to a new place where you knew nothing about the community. Where they were all used to this radio station I'd never heard.

Do you know what I mean?

No? Fine.

We went to the Great Southern.

I checked in while Carmel rang home.

That hotel smell.

Dinner was from seven.

We went to our room. Thick carpet and a big bed. We swam in the deserted pool.

The chlorine in the air when we got dressed.

We had a few pints in the plush bar and made our way leisurely for a late meal.

If Carmel was unaccustomed to luxury, she didn't show it.

She had assurance.

Which annoyed the fuck out of me.

We had a few more drinks. And we were too tired or too full to fuck.

And if you stay in a hotel, you've got to fuck.

So I made a point of waking up early.

We drove home Sunday.

I was refreshed and content.

After dropping Carmel off I went for a few beers with Tony Reagan, our professor.

The famous philosopher, Wolfgang Konigsberg, was visiting our department that week.

He was only giving three lectures.

The department had agreed to this but I wanted the chance of a question and answer session where we could discuss his ideas. I knew I could have this guy on the ropes if I had the opportunity to press him, not that I was particularly interested in his area.

Tony said we could talk about it, next day, at the Monday morning staff meeting.

That night I slept the sleep of the just and righteous and all that kind of shit.

The next morning I sat in my office looking at all my beautiful books.

Sometimes I'd go to the library late at night and just sit in between the shelves. Breathing in all those years of useless discussion.

I was working on a book I knew no one was going to read.

What would be the point?

My office was on a corner of the highest part of the college.

This tickled Tony Reagan no end.

He said that the philosophy department was near heaven so that when the questions became too unbearable we could lean out the window and ask God.

Poor Tony was a terrible gobshite.

I sorted out two lectures I wasn't looking forward to giving that afternoon and I went to the staff meeting.

Tony Reagan always wanted to please everyone.

The rationalists, the empiricists, me.

This was a pity because we were just a bunch of selfish children and it wasn't worth it.

He should have just treated us like shit and told us to get on with the philosophy.

But there you are.

The first argument was about who should pick Konigsberg up from the airport.

This took about half an hour.

Trish Meehan was the acknowledged expert on his work, but she was relatively new and Reagan wanted someone who'd represent the department better.

This turned into a squabble.

In the end, six of us were to be at the airport in three cars.

This was lunacy but I kept my mouth shut.

I was waiting for the big picture.

I knew I could fuck Konigsberg up.

Trish Meehan objected to him having to get involved in a discussion, because he was nearly ninety and would already be exhausted from his lectures.

But she was just being a contrary bollocks because she knew no one would touch her with a ten-foot pole. She was taking it out on the world.

I ranted on and on about how undemocratic this was, not to mention the importance of discussion to the progress of ideas, blah blah de blah blah.

Well I might as well have hopped up on the table and taken a dump for all the good it did.

They won, I lost and I fucking hate losing.

The only thing I could salvage was the satisfaction of making Tony Reagan feel bad by pretending to be really upset.

I got up, threw everything into my briefcase, and said I didn't see the point in continuing the pursuit of truth and knowledge in these conditions and some other swine could corrupt the kids in my lectures that afternoon, because I certainly wouldn't.

I gave Trish Meehan the finger on the sly, and I stormed out, slamming the door.

Half day.

Lovely.

FRANK

I had never held one before and I was surprised at how heavy it was.

The barrel had been sawn in half and the wood in the stock was chipped and cracked.

He didn't give me any cartridges.

I asked him when he wanted it back but he just smiled and told me to get rid of it when I was finished.

He was going away and he told me to wish him luck. I did and off he went.

We weren't open yet.

I sat there with the bag at a table.

I thought I was going to have a heart attack. But I felt brilliant at the same time. It was like I could hear and see everything very clearly.

Like I could solve anything by thinking.

It was a feeling of power.

I put the gun upstairs and got on with my work.

Dad joked with me.

He wanted to know if I'd been drinking—I was in that good a mood.

But he was the one who'd had a drink.

He was under so much pressure.

His face was gray.

I hated looking at him in daylight.

His skin hung around him like a coat on a hook.

I thought the fucking eejit was great.

I was going to do something for him.

I waited till things eased off about half two. Dad was reading the paper.

I went upstairs and got my stuff.

I had cut eyeholes in one of Joe's bobble hats. I'd cut the bobble off as well.

I was going to ask him if I could borrow one, but he was in a funny mood.

I had an old parka jacket and a pair of tracksuit bottoms.

I put the hat on and shoved the shotgun down my pants.

Then I ran down and out the back.

Dad never saw me.

I went across the yard and checked the street. No one about.

I went left down to the seafront and right past the few houses before Simple Simon's.

The street was deserted.

I pulled Joe's hat down over my face and I yanked the gun out.

I took a few deep breaths and walked straight in.

No one noticed me at first.

Charlie was sitting on a stool watching the TV.

Tim Byrne, one of the clerks, was reading the *Irish Independent* and picking his nose.

Two auldfellas were filling out a docket with a stubby pencil.

And the man himself, Simple Simon McFucking Bollocks, walked out from behind the counter with a cup of tea.

"Alright," I said.

Simon dropped his cup and Charlie fell off the stool.

Tim Byrne put his hands up and the two auldfellas started arguing about the second horse in a treble.

It was easier than I thought it was going to be.

I got everyone to lie on the floor of the shop, then I locked the door.

I told Simple Simon to give me every penny in the place.

He said it wasn't much and it wouldn't be worth my while.

He kept calling me "Son."

I pulled him up and stuck the gun between his legs.

He went white and did a shit in his pants.

I was smiling behind the hat.

He was telling me to take it easy.

I let him go and he sort of waddled behind the counter.

I jumped up on it so I could watch him and keep an eye on the others.

He pulled about thirty quid out of the till and I took it.

Then I said, "And the safe." I didn't even know if he had a safe.

But sure enough, he nearly started to cry and went towards the office.

"Leave the door open," I told him.

He was kneeling on the floor.

Charlie was glaring up at me with his little piggy eyes.

I was terrified of him. But he just lay there.

Then Simon came back out with two big envelopes.

I leapt off the counter and stuck them in my pockets.

Then I told Simon to take his clothes off.

Naturally, he refused.

But I stuck the gun under his chin and he slowly unbut-
toned his pants.

He was shaking so much I thought he was going to have a fit.

I nearly felt sorry for him, standing there with his tits like
a girl.

I took him by the hair and we went to the door. I undid the
latch and made sure there was no one around.

I waited for a car to turn the corner at Reynolds and I
pulled Simon out with me and slammed the door behind us.

I could hear him thumping and shouting to be let back in.
And I was around the corner like a shot.

I ran through the yard at the back of the bookies and over
to the wall that adjoins the lane. There was a bin and I used
it to get up and grab the top of the wall.

And then I nearly collapsed when I heard someone shouting.

Charlie was running towards me.

I fucked the gun over the wall and threw my leg up.

I caught my heel at the top and heaved myself over. The ground was lower on the far side and I fell in a heap.

I could hear Charlie getting up on the bin. I shoved the gun into my pants and started running down the lane.

I pulled Joe's hat off and the gun slipped down my leg. I grabbed it and limped past the back of Creevan's butchers.

I got out on to Main Street and headed for Super Value.

I had to get in somewhere before Charlie came out of the lane.

I could have gone into Mary Kennedy's pub but I never drank there and they'd have been talking about the time I came in for years.

It was too suspicious.

I was trying to walk normally and breathe slowly. Nobody paid me any heed.

But Super Value was too far away.

I was going to be caught.

And then Ray pulled over and gave me a lift.

(Interval.)

JOE

That Sunday and Monday have to have been the two
weirdest days of my life.

Frank didn't say anything about what he'd told me on Friday
night, and to tell you the truth I'd forgotten about it.

I thought he was drunk.

Sunday started off normal enough.

Carmel was away with Ray, and Dad and Frank did the dinner.

They'd sort of taken over Mam's jobs about four years
before, when she got really sick.

At the time I could remember her dinners and I knew that
the new ones were different.

But now I couldn't remember.

I couldn't go to see her much.

I just couldn't.

One time she didn't know who I was and she got a fright
when Dad told her.

She was roaring crying.

It was sick. I couldn't stand it.

I was glad when she died.

I had gotten used to her not being at home.

I didn't want to waste time getting upset. It wasn't my fault.

I didn't talk about her and I didn't like thinking about her. It scared me.

And that was all there was to it.

So anyway, after dinner on Sunday I was watching a brutal film and I was going to go up to my room, when the phone rang.

It was Damien.

There was a tickle in my stomach.

He wanted to know if I was going to Shadows.

It was a disco out near the dual carriageway.

Behind the Ancient Mariner bar.

I'd never been there and I knew my dad wouldn't let me go.

The Mariner was called the "Bucket of Blood" because of all the fights and a barman had lost a finger once, trying to kick someone out.

Dad said it was full of gobshites and knackers.

Frank said that Shadows was crap and that the bouncers spent the whole night kicking people out, because they didn't refuse anyone. To get their money.

The bouncers would have to kick in the cubicle doors in the jacks and pull couples out who were having a quick shag.

But Frank hadn't gone there in years.

I told Damien I'd go if he was, but I had no ID and you had to be eighteen because there was a bar.

Damien said they never looked for ID if you looked anywhere near sixteen or so.

He asked me if I wanted him to get me some cans because he was going to the off licence. It was a good idea to get pissed before you went in, because the pints were £2.50.

I told him I wanted cans. But I didn't know how many to get. I didn't know how many made you drunk.

I thought I'd aim high and told him to get me ten. He laughed and told me to stop messing. But I didn't know if that meant I should ask for more or less, so I asked how many he was getting.

He said four or five. I said to get me the same.

But then he said, "What do you want?" And I said, "Four." And he said, "Four what?" And I said, "Four cans." "Of what?" he said.

I said "Carlsberg." Advertising works.

We arranged to meet at the monument in the Christian Brothers' school where all the lunatics went.

I had to decide what to wear.

I had no good clothes.

In the end I took one of Frank's shirts.

It was black with a white pattern.

Little birds.

Actually I saw it again recently.

Stupid-looking thing.

I had a shower and put on loads of talc.

I cut myself shaving, and when I put Frank's new aftershave on, my face went all red and angry. I looked like there was something wrong with me.

Which was unfair because I was right as rain.

I got my bike out and told Dad I was calling for Fergus and Noel.

The air was frosty and there was an orange glow over the city.

But out by us you could see the stars.

I knew Damien would be late because he always was.

I locked my bike at the bottom of the monument and went up about a hundred steps to where you could sit down.

It was a great view.

In the distance I could see Dublin Bay.

All the lights. It was very peaceful.

I thought about what my wife would be like.

But she just seemed to be like me and it got a bit boring.

After about half an hour, I saw Damien coming through the gates. He had a bag with him.

He was far away and very small.

I thought that if I'd had a gun I could have shot him.

I don't know what made me think that.

He was quite drunk already.

He sat beside me and I was asking him about Shadows.

He told me that if I didn't get my end away, he'd give me a hundred quid.

He had had a bottle of wine with his mum before coming out.

I thought that was great.

Then I thought about my mum.

She would never have drunk a bottle of wine with anyone.

I was a bit nervous about drinking the Carlsberg. I had had beer a few times at home and I'd liked it.

Dad put lemonade in it.

After two cans I'd felt happier than I'd ever felt. I was in love with Damien—in a friendly way.

I wanted him to myself, if that's what love is.

I couldn't finish my last can.

We went down to our bikes and we were laughing at nothing.

We wobbled all over the road.

There was a huge queue outside Shadows.

We were waiting for about twenty minutes.

The girls had miniskirts or leggings but only a few had nice legs.

There was too much perfume everywhere.

It was in my mouth.

The blokes looked like they'd kill you as soon as look at you.

The bouncers wouldn't let a group of fellas in. They were barred.

They started shouting and saying the bouncers were fucking dead.

I couldn't see what the big deal was.

It looked like the sort of place I'd prefer to be barred from.

When we got in we were searched.

And we had to pay six fucking quid.

The music was brutal. I was made to put my jacket in the cloakroom, and I had to pay fifty pence.

There was pink fluorescent tubing all along the walls and around the dance floor.

I was trying not to catch anyone's eye in case I got a hiding.

Damien got a drink at the bar.

He knew some girls there.

I saw him dancing.

The place got packed really quickly.

I was getting tired.

I walked around and watched everything.

There was a stool at the bar so I sat there.

But then I had to buy a drink.

I got a pint of Carlsberg.

It made me feel better.

I saw a bloke who was about twenty.

He looked like he did weights.

He was on his own dancing at the bar.

He was on something.

A girl came over to him and they started getting off. Then she got off with someone else. It was mad.

It was a shithole.

Everyone behaved like animals.

I had quite a lot of principles.

At about eleven Damien came over to me.

He was holding a girl around the waist.

She was thin and she had dyed blond hair.

She was smiling but she was very drunk.

Damien asked if I was ready to go.

Too fucking right I was, I told him.

He laughed.

He brought the girl out with us.

He was getting off with her while I unlocked the bikes.

She wanted us to walk her home.

She lived up near the Grange where all the knackers lived.

We walked down the dual carriageway.

They kept stopping and kissing.

We turned up by the garden center.

There was a lane that ran up along the side of a hill.

It was really dark but it was a short cut for the Grange.

We had to go up by the old church with no roof that everyone said was haunted.

Damien told me to hang on.

The girl was nearly asleep and he took her into the graveyard.

I just wanted to go home.

I waited a few minutes because I thought they were going to the toilet.

But I got pissed off and went in to get them.

I saw something moving on a grave.

I nearly shit myself because I thought it was something crawling out of the grave.

But it was worse.

Damien had his trousers down and the girl's legs were on either side of him, like they were broken.

Her neck was on the low rail around the grave and her head hung over the gravel.

Damien was pushing into her like he wanted to put her in the ground.

I ran straight back to my bike and cycled home.

I said good night and got sick in the bathroom.

I wondered if the girl knew what was happening to her. I wanted to hop on my bike and go back.

But it was too late. It was pointless.

I lay in bed and I dreamed.

I saw the girl, and I saw the girl I fancied, Deborah Something, and I saw another woman in a red dress with no shoes on.

She was laughing at herself.

I woke up at four in the morning.

I stood in the kitchen drinking juice.

The horrible thing was that what I saw made me sick to my stomach, but at the same time it was really turning me on.

And that upset me.

I was in bits all that Monday in school.

Damien never came in.

I had to see him.

I wanted him to tell me the girl had a great time and he saw her home.

I didn't want to hear anything else.

I couldn't concentrate on anything.

When I got home, Dad was reading the paper.

I didn't want to speak to anybody.

I went straight to my room.

Frank and Ray were sitting on my bed.

And all over Frank's bed was the biggest load of money I'd ever seen.

RAY

It was the most bizarre fucking situation.

Head-the-Ball was after doing an armed robbery. And I'd done the getaway.

He was going mad with excitement. And I have to admit, it was fairly catching.

I was glad when Joe found us in the room because it made Frank act a bit more responsibly.

He was very straight and told Joe everything.

Joe was annoyed.

He wasn't sure whether or not Frank was taking the piss. He just didn't want to believe it. But you could see he did.

And he was shitting himself.

And this was getting on Frank's nerves and he wanted to get out of the house.

I told him he should just get back to work and pretend everything was normal.

But Frank was going mad.

So I said we could go for a quick drive.

Frank hid the money under his bed.

He had a suitcase there where he kept bits and pieces.

He'd gotten nearly thirty grand.

He made Joe come with us to make sure he didn't do anything stupid, and then we couldn't resist it, we drove by the bookies.

There were two squad cars parked outside and a guard was standing in the doorway.

A group of women had come out of their houses and they had their arms folded, talking about it.

It had only taken Frank about five minutes and he was sure no one had seen him.

No one was going to believe he'd done it anyway.

He kept telling it over and over and turning the radio on and off.

Joe was quiet at first, but then he started asking questions.

We drove along the coast.

Frank and Joe started to laugh at the whole thing.

Lunatics. But we all had different natures.

For now I was happy to roll along merrily and not get too upset.

I don't get upset much.

But the more Joe was asking what we should do next, the more I was beginning to see what a good fucking question it was.

I have that sort of philosophical training.

So after driving around for a while I decided that enough was enough.

It was getting a bit stupid.

I pulled over and told them what to do.

Absolutely nothing.

They had to go back and pretend nothing had happened. Listen to what people said, what the local theories were, and cultivate them.

They had to see which way the cookie bounced.

The last thing they wanted to do was a Thelma and Louise job.

Only a stupid prick would take off.

In a way, I wanted them off my back.

I didn't need the hassle.

So we went back to the chipper, and of course, I was right.

There wasn't a stir in the place.

Why would there be?

No guards had come. No nothing.

I had a bite with Joe and Frank got back to work.

People were coming in for their tea and asking Frank if he'd heard about the bookies.

And Frank was all, "Yeah, what happened exactly?"

And the stories were all different.

Someone said it was a gang of raiders who'd gotten away in a car.

Someone else said the robbers had a stick of dynamite and they'd threatened to blow up the safe if McCurdie didn't open it.

Some fucking eejit with a woolly hat said a shot had been fired into the ceiling and the guards were looking for finger-prints on the bullet.

Joe was laughing but Frank kept a straight face. And I knew he'd be okay.

And later on when Carmel came home, we went up to her room.

What a beautiful girl she was.

What a fit girl.

Well.

In the morning there was a message on my machine from Tony Reagan.

He wanted to apologize for what had happened at the staff meeting.

He hoped I understood that it was Konigsberg who'd insisted on giving his papers with no discussion.

There was very little Tony could do but he would try to have a word.

I rang him back. I was gracious and I told him not to worry.

When I got into my office there was a note slipped under the door.

It was from the third-year I'd slept with. She had wanted to meet me the night before. Well, too late now.

I fucked it in the bin.

I didn't have her in any classes that week and I'm going to be completely frank with you here. I didn't really like her.

And I have the guts to admit that, you know?

I took out the two books of collected papers I had by Konigsberg.

He had been developing this brutal theory since the fifties.

He said that language was an organic thing, like any plant or animal. And just like any plant or animal, it was born, lived healthily for a while, making other little languages, like its offspring, and then it died. Same as everything else.

And our language is dying now.

No one talks properly.

There is a lack of sincerity, he claimed, because language is sick now.

It isn't vital enough to sustain validity.

Politicians are elected on saying the right thing strategically, not morally.

People in general aren't reading.

The action movie has replaced poetry.

People can't make an effort to be entertained.

They take drugs instead.

Blah, blah, blah, language is dying.

Now this meant that Konigsberg was either very clever or very lucky.

Because it made him hard to categorize.

He was a sort of Aristotelian, Darwinian, Marxist, Communitarian type thing.

And I don't know how much money he'd made hawking this notion around the lecture circuit. But I'd say it would have to be something pretty fucking amazing.

Tony Reagan knocked in to see me.

He'd just been on to Konigsberg's personal secretary or agent, or whatever she was.

And lo and behold, he had agreed to a very brief question and answer session after his last lecture.

I told Tony I owed him one.

But he said he was looking forward to it.

It'd be entertaining to say the least.

But I knew if I could nail Konigsberg, they'd be writing articles about me for years.

When he finally arrived, there was a big buzz in the college.

You see, nearly every department found him relevant— literature, linguistics, history, philosophy, everybody.

They had his first lecture in the evening so all the students would get a chance to see him.

He was in the largest lecture theatre but it was so full they had to rig up a closed-circuit system to the next theatre, where everyone could see him on a huge screen.

With the question and answer session not happening till the third lecture I wasn't bothered going to the first two.

Anyway the thought of watching all those morons slobber-ing all over Konigsberg annoyed me.

And it made me jealous. I admit it.

It did.

There was a sort of reception thing after each lecture, which I did go to.

There was free wine and sandwiches.

Konigsberg was never there.

He needed his rest. Only postgraduates were supposed to be at these receptions and there were academics from all over Europe there especially.

But a bunch of philosophy students who were in with the department always blagged their way in to get locked.

So you had to be quick.

I got completely rat-arsed and all around me twits tried to be clever and funny.

I made a point of getting into a row and left. On the way home I phoned Frank to get the lowdown.

Everything was cool.

People saw the robbery as one of those things that happen, and that's life and it was a learning experience and that was that.

But at the same time, Frank was nervous and excited and he wanted to do something.

He wanted to unwind. He wanted to get away.

I didn't want him doing anything thick so I told him we could drive down the country at the weekend. Me, him and Joe.

That way I could keep an eye on them.

Konigsberg's last lecture was on Friday morning and I arranged to pick them up after that.

That was the plan.

On Thursday night, I was at another wine and shite-talk reception.

A bottle and a half into the proceedings and I spot the third-year chick.

And she was pretending not to see me.

I ask you.

And may God forgive me, but with every glass of Earnest and Julio Gallo, her tits were getting more imperative.

So I fucked over to the student bar with her and her bunch of know-it-all shitbrain friends.

And there we are, pint after pint and she's sitting beside me with her great big legs in knee-high boots.

And I'm getting a dirty mind and I know that if I don't get it in her in the next few minutes, I'm going to give someone a dig.

So we split and I'm giving her a lift home.

And her hand is down my pants and I open them up and Jesus Christ, she's sucking me like a starving baby.

So we get to her place, I'm fucked.

She carries me up the stairs into her room.

And I remember I was really interested in her keeping her boots on.

And I was just pulling off her knickers and the door burst open.

And this little fellow with long hair ran in, going berserk.

He jumped on me and she was shouting, "Vyvyan, No!" He pushes me out into the landing.

I was trying to pull my pants up, and I fell down the stairs onto the hall table.

The phone flew off and went through the glass in the front door.

And I needn't tell you, I was out into the car like a bullet.

I locked my door and your man was banging on the roof. I reversed at about fifty miles an hour. I didn't even look.

I skidded across the street and got it into first. Vyvyan jumps in front of the car.

I put the foot down.

I'm not sure, but I think I might have clipped him. I wasn't going back to check.

I had a big day in the morning.

I was getting an early night.

When I got home I threw some stuff into a bag for going away with the boys.

Then I lay in the bath and I was dreaming about Martha Nussbaum.

We were talking about Aristotle and getting ready to go to bed for a shag and she lifted up her dress and she had a dick.

I jumped and woke up.

It was nearly two o'clock in the morning and the bath was freezing.

I poured myself a large glass of medicinal brandy, went to bed and shivered myself to sleep.

The alarm went off.

Ten o'clock.

Konigsberg's lecture was at eleven.

And Jesus Christ, early night or not, after all the wine and beer and brandy, not to mention lying in a cold bath for half the night, I was completely bollocks.

I had an hour, but I could hardly fucking move.

I had a shower and a shave.

Tried to have a shit but nothing was happening.

I was in bits.

On the way into college I stopped for petrol and got some solphadene and juice.

I put the carton to my mouth and I swear to God I couldn't stop drinking until the entire liter was gone. I was that dehydrated.

The lecture theatre was full of nobodies all out for as much enlightenment as their little heads could handle.

And there he was.

Professor Wolfgang Konigsberg was about five foot and completely bald.

He sounded like Spike Milligan doing Hitler impressions. I could hardly hear what he was saying.

It was giving me a headache.

Everyone was watching him intently.

Some were even nodding in agreement, going, "Mmm, mmm."

It would make you sick.

The third-year chick was looking over at me. She was sobbing into a little piece of toilet roll.

I was beginning to feel worse.

There was a gurgling sound coming from my stomach. There were waves of nausea.

I was sweating but my feet were freezing.

I closed my eyes.

Then there was applause and I heard Tony Reagan say, "Professor Konigsberg has very kindly agreed to take one or two questions. And I know that Dr. Raymond Sullivan would like to ask the first one."

That was me.

My eyes were watering.

My head felt lighter than my body.

And I was sitting in the middle of a row.

I couldn't get out.

Everyone looked at me expectantly.

Konigsberg was looking around, wondering who was going to say something.

And then, absolutely beyond my control, a long stream of orange puke shot out of my mouth.

It sailed across the room and all over the people for about ten feet in front of me.

I spluttered for a moment, and coughed a little, and then there was complete silence.

I immediately felt much better.

I wiped my face and looked around.

No one could believe what they had just seen.

I stood up and cleared my throat.

"Yes. Thank you, Professor Reagan," I said. "I would like to ask Professor Konigsberg if, during his long and eminent career, he has ever seen anything quite like that."

Tony Reagan didn't know what to do.

He just looked at Konigsberg.

The smell of sick was rising through the room.

Konigsberg didn't say anything.

And then, finally, he slowly shook his head.

I thanked him politely and made my way out.

I couldn't even remember what I had wanted to say.

Fuck it.

FRANK (*To Ray*)

I never heard that.

RAY

I've been saving it.

FRANK

It was a weird feeling.

I had thirty thousand pounds under my bed.

The first thing I did, the evening of the robbery, was bury the gun.

I took it up to the hill before the Grange and dug a hole under a tree in the woods.

I wasn't sure what to do with the money though. I didn't want to bury it in case it was too hard to get when I needed it.

And I was afraid to lodge it in case some case I knew at the bank got suspicious.

I was even afraid to look at it.

So it just lay there under the bed.

But no one was on to me and that was obvious.

About the Wednesday, Simple Simon and Charlie came in for their lunch.

They were very quiet.

They'd lost their swagger.

I was a smart arse.

I was all, "Do you think they'll catch whoever did it, Mr. McCurdie?"

And he was, "I don't honestly think so, Frank, I really don't."

Charlie couldn't understand how the robber had disappeared after running down the lane.

"I nearly had the bastard, Frank," he said. "I was about as close to him as I am to you now." Which was too fucking true.

Simon was telling Charlie not to blame himself. There was nothing he could have done. And I was agreeing with them.

But I was sick to the gills when I thought about how lucky I'd been.

If Ray hadn't come I was fucked.

And what good had it done?

How could I pay Dad's loan off?

Everyone would know it was me.

I was getting restless.

Joe was moping around in the dumps all the time and I couldn't cheer him up.

I was hoping it wasn't my fault.

But sometimes you have to decide that principles will only fuck you up, because no one else is ever moral.

I wanted to give Joe some cash.

I didn't know what I wanted.

When we were in bed one night, I said I hoped he wasn't angry at me.

But he wasn't.

He told me about seeing some eejit from his school having it off with a knacker from the Grange. It had really upset him.

But I couldn't see the big deal and I didn't know what to say to him.

I was annoyed at him.

But then that night I was thinking about a woman I knew when I was Joe's age.

I used to wash her windows and cut the grass.

She had two young children and her husband was a plumber.

I sometimes used to walk with her to collect her kids from school.

And then one day, in her kitchen, she touched my hand and I never went back.

I was going to tell Joe this, but he was asleep. I didn't see what it had to do with him anyway.

I decided we should get away for a few days.

I asked Ray. His car would give us that aimless millionaire feeling I was after.

I told Carmel I wanted her to work with Dad for the weekend.

She went bananas because she had an exam coming up. But I told her that Joe needed a break from his studying and she could be a Christian for five minutes.

That got her. She was guilty about Joe not having a mother, and she was always fighting with him.

I know it was mean, but she felt it and you've got to use what you've got.

I waited until Dad was into the second half of the bottle before I said anything.

He smiled. He thought it was a good idea.

What a great man. He made me proud.

I couldn't leave the money under the bed for the weekend. So me and Joe put it all into plastic bags with some stones, then we sealed them with elastic bands and put them in the tank up in the attic.

And when we came back down, it hit us that we should have taken some out for the weekend. We got all giggly and we were wondering how much we should take.

We didn't know, so we guessed on five grand.

Joe was cheering up.

I told him not to go into school on Friday because Ray would be picking us up at lunchtime.

In the morning I was washing the floor and the old man came over and handed me fifty quid. Of course, I was saying, "No, no." But he wouldn't take it back. "For a drink," he kept saying. "Buy a round." Then he winked at me and walked off.

It was the first time I'd felt guilty.

That man had done everything by the rules in his life and look what happened.

He was left on his own and shagged by bastards like McCurdie.

But he was right. That was the thing.

Well I didn't want to be right anymore.

That's a load of meaningless toss.

I was glad when Ray showed up.

He looked like shit.

He was having a whiskey with Dad while I went to get changed.

Joe came in and told me Dad had given him twenty quid. He felt really guilty as well.

We broke our shit laughing.

We put the gear in the car and we were trying to decide where to go.

We hadn't thought about it.

Joe just said, "Cork," and that was it.

We were off.

It felt good to be moving.

We were taking the piss out of Marian Finucane on the radio.

They were going on about planning permission for sheds and extensions.

Ray said he'd give her shed an extension if she didn't shut the fuck up.

He had it in for everybody.

He was in bad humor because he was hungover.

So we stopped in Abbeyleix for a cure.

I wasn't sure how to treat Joe in this respect. But he just asked us what we wanted and bought the first round.

I was relieved.

The last thing I wanted was to have to be his parent.
He had to grow up. Let him.

It was very nice there and we didn't want to go. But Cork it was, and off we went.

I asked Ray which was the most expensive hotel. We could afford it.

Me and Joe shared a room.

Old habits.

And Ray got himself a double room, because, as he put it, you never know.

Joe was having a bath and I took Ray aside to give him a grand for the weekend.

He didn't want it, but I made him take it. We were like children playing.

We had a drink sent up to the room and Ray toasted me.

He said I was the weirdest bastard he'd ever met.

At nine we went down and had a beautiful dinner. We got champagne, but only Ray liked it. Me and Joe thought it was horrible.

Ray said we were the typical nouveau riche, all money and no taste.

Fuck him. We had pints.

Afterwards we headed into town.

Most of the pubs were packed but we found a little auldfellas place that served us till about half twelve.

Back at the hotel there was a disco.

We got a drink and Ray started talking to a girl around Joe's age, and I don't know what he said to her, maybe he paid her, I don't know. But she came over, asked Joe to dance and got off with him the whole evening.

Joe was beaming when we went to bed.

But then he said he missed her.

Everything backfires.

You can't do fucking anything.

And that was what the weekend was like.

We were the boys.

Rested and refreshed.

Until we got back on Sunday evening and there was a squad car outside the chipper.

JOE

When we saw the guards, I think we all had the same idea.

To put the foot down and get out of there.

But it was too late. They saw us.

It was horrible.

Ray pulled over and a sergeant asked us to come in.

There was a detective sitting with Dad in the front room.
Dad looked wrecked.

Carmel glared at us.

Frank was white and his hands were shaking.

But we were all completely wrong.

Because it was me the detective wanted to talk to. He asked
me if I knew a girl called Sarah Comisky.

I didn't, I'd never heard the name.

Then he asked me if I ever went to Shadows nightclub.

I looked at Dad, but I had to say yes.

He asked was I there the previous Sunday.

I said I was and he nodded.

He just wanted to talk to me and Dad.

Everyone else had to go.

And when they were gone, he said I'd been accused of
raping Sarah Comisky.

I nearly fell on the floor.

I said it wasn't me.

I didn't know any Sarahs.

But the detective told me to relax.

The girl hadn't accused me.

Damien had.

She had been attacked up in the graveyard near the Grange.

She had identified Damien as her attacker, but he said it was
me.

The girl was very drunk but she did remember someone else being there.

So the guards wanted to find out if both of us had done it, or if one, which one.

Dad came with me down to the station and I had to give my account of what had happened. They made sure I got all the details right and then they gave me a cup of tea and a KitKat.

Then Dad signed something, then I did and they took a blood test.

Then we could go home.

I couldn't believe Damien had dropped me in it like that.

But Dad said I was too naive and that people would do anything to save their skin.

He said he knew it was disappointing but that was the way it was.

At home we all sat up late and talked about it and everyone was great.

We all drank beer until very late in the morning.

In bed that night I thought about my mother. It wasn't about the times when she couldn't talk and gave me nightmares.

It was about another time I'd forgotten.

Dad was teaching me how to skim stones on the beach. And Mum was trying to do it and she couldn't.

It was summer and she had a red dress on.

Dad was slagging her and she was laughing at herself.

And I felt safe and the safe feeling stayed.

I didn't go to school that week and the guards called on Tuesday to say that my test was negative.

They were charging Damien.

There was a bit of a shindig in the house.

Frank told me he was putting money away for me to go to college, but I wasn't to say anything to Dad.

And Frank went to Chicago a few weeks later and he sent money back for Dad to pay off his loan.

Maybe he had a job, maybe he didn't.

Dad wasn't to know.

Ray brought a book out which nobody read.

But he was pleased.

He said that that was the point.

So in the end it was like things started off good, and just got better.

Is that cheating?

I don't know.

It's hard to say.

I can still see the girl.

End of Play

THE
GOOD THIEF

For Kevin Hely and Rionach

The Good Thief was first performed under the title *The Light of Jesus* at the City Arts Centre, Dublin, on April 18, 1994 by The Fly by Night Theatre Company. It was performed by Kevin Hely, with slide photography by Paul Kinsella. It was directed by Conor McPherson.

The play was subsequently performed as part of the Dublin Theatre Festival on October 4, 1994. It was a Loopline production, designed by Anne Layde. It was performed by Garrett Keogh, with slide photography by Robbie Ryan. It was directed by Conor McPherson.

Let's begin with an incident.

I was sitting in Joe Murray's bar one night, as I usually did.

I was talking to this couple I liked and having a few beers.

I was working for Joe Murray at this time as a paid thug.

I scared people for him.

Set fire to places.

Shot people. As warnings.

My girlfriend Greta had just left me but I still saw her most days because she had left me for Joe Murray.

Power attracts women.

Also, I had been beating her up and I knew it was wrong but I'm not the issue here, so let's leave it.

Let's not. She annoyed me.

She gave herself to any man who wanted it. I knew this for a fact and I was sick of sticking it where someone else had had it a few hours ago.

Anyway, I was having a few glasses of beer with this couple I really liked and relaxing.

That day I'd had to chase a man up and down his premises in Capel Street.

He knew all these stairwells and stuff you wouldn't think were there.

I was exhausted.

He was a shoe repairman.

I hate people with skills who can do stuff.

It's a small quibble but I refuse to constrain my personality.

I believe that that can lead to problems.

I must've broken every bone in his hands.

Then I shaved his head and kicked his nuts so many times he passed out.

This couple I was talking to were young and funny.

They came in and out sometimes.

They were friendly with each other too.

I was a little bit jealous of them but I was happy for them at the same time.

I was just having a few glasses of beer and we were chatting about politics and movies and the weather and stuff.

I saw Greta over the other side of the bar talking to Harry Delaney, a man who'd been living in England for a number of years and wore a necklace.

I felt like tossing my drink over at them but I was in too good a mood.

The couple I was talking to bought me a drink and I bought them one and we were talking about clothes and style.

Greta walked past me and didn't look.

She had her coat on and she was smoking.

I saw Harry Delaney shoot back his drink and go the long way 'round.

I knew what they were doing.

I was going mad but, Fuck them, I thought.

It was a cold night.

They'd have to do it in the car park.

They'd freeze their bare arses off.

And Greta would have to be back at closing time to suck Joe Murray's dick. Or whatever it was she did after hours.

I'm probably not being very fair.

But life's not fair.

So she was gone out with Harry Delaney and she was gone a few minutes.

I was shooting the breeze with this young couple I really liked and Joe Murray comes downstairs and starts looking around.

The look on his face made my day.

When he saw that Greta wasn't there he looked miserable and annoyed at the same time.

You see, I knew he loved Greta.

He was the type of man who would've put her in a china cabinet and polish her if he could.

But I knew what he liked.

He liked putting it up girls' arses and I'd seen him do it.

He was a right degenerate.

This was one of the things annoyed me about him and Greta. She probably enjoyed it. I always preferred it straight.

I'm not a messer.

He was looking around and people were talking to him. Asking him for favors or spoofing him he'd lost weight.

Eventually I heard him ask somebody where Greta was, but no one had seen her go out.

He came around to us and I introduced everyone. The young couple were leaving.

I said I'd see them again and it was nice talking to them.

Murray bought me a drink and began talking a bit of business.

But I knew he was going to talk to me about Greta.

He had never squared it with me, the way she'd moved out of our place and into his.

I knew that if he mentioned it, it would annoy me too much.

He asked me had I seen her.

I said I had but I didn't know where she was.

Then it was sort of funny.

He said, "Does she do this much? I mean go off without saying anything?"

I thought it was gas. Him asking me this.

It was very bad manners but I answered him anyway and said I didn't know.

I could see he knew he shouldn't have asked me for advice after taking her away from me. But sometimes he was as thick as shit. He really was.

Yeah.

Well. That's the incident I wanted to begin with. It's sort of funny, isn't it? Kind of sick as well.

There's just something not quite right about it. Hard to put your finger on though.

Anyway, something about it changed the way I felt about Joe Murray and the way I felt probably contributed to the mayhem that happened over the next few days.

And that's what I really want to talk about.

So that night I had a couple of beers after closing with Joe Murray and Vinnie Rourke, an old-time vicious bastard who'd done fifteen years for armed robbery.

I didn't speak to him much and I'd heard he had "mellowed with age."

But I knew he was a psycho and that he did odd jobs for Murray when he wanted a real pro and not a messy bastard like me.

Greta came back and Murray was asking her where she'd been and where Harry Delaney was. But she didn't answer him. She just poured herself a big tequila and lit a cigarette.

Vinnie Rourke and a little fucker who followed him everywhere, Seamus Parker, were looking at her like they wanted to give her one each. Or at the same time.

Joe Murray always seemed weak when Greta was around.

I was imagining Murray doing it to her and her loving it. It disgusted me but I couldn't get it out of my head.

I had to bang a couple of shorts away.

I was messing with the jukebox, putting the Beatles on.

Murray came over and gave me a piece of paper with an address on it. It was a man called Mitchell who owned a number of warehouses which he leased to food importers mostly. But we also knew that from time to time he'd hold on to dodgy gear from some of the bigger robberies in the city. Antiques and that.

Murray had been threatening to set fire to Mitchell's warehouses for years.

This brought in about a grand and a half a month, but with the recession Mitchell was asking for some leeway.

Murray had refused and Mitchell was giving it all this guff about some second cousin in the IRA getting on to it.

My job was to go 'round to his house and scare him.

I told Murray okay and he gave me a hundred as a sub.

Back at the bar, Vinnie Rourke was staring at me. I knew that he didn't like Murray giving me work for some reason.

But I did my best to ignore him and put plenty of effort into drinking Greta out of my head.

It got hazy after that and I just remember driving home wishing I was more drunk.

When I woke up it was about nine and I had a blinder of a hangover.

I considered not doing the job for Murray but he had given me a sub and that meant it was important to him.

I did a trick from my days as a second lieutenant which always fooled my body into action.

First I took some aspirin and then some vivioptal tablets which are a tonic, giving you energy after you've been sick, then a valium, and then I put the kettle on.

I ran a cold bath while I shaved, then I stripped and hitting the water was like being born. Everything went mad. I put my head under the water and blew bubbles.

Then I stood up and let my body get warm before sliding under for another shock.

I was shivering while I dried myself.

I made a huge hot whiskey with lemon and cloves and it blew the roof off my head.

Made me drunk very quickly.

I had another one and then I checked my guns.

The shotgun I had was beautifully handmade by a man in Mullingar, but of course I'd ruined it by sawing the barrel in half.

It was lethal and it often frightened me to carry it. I was always worried it would go off.

I also had a very old, very beautiful Webley revolver which was more just in case. I was told that this one I had was used to give the coup de grâce to deserters in France. I never knew if that was true.

It was accurate up to about sixty yards and it was so pristine I doubted it had ever seen action.

It was starting to rain as I got into the car. I wanted to get this over with quickly before my hangover caught up with me.

There was only old tat on the radio but I kept it on for company.

When I was nearly there I took my bag of gear out.

I had a balaclava for extra frighteners and an industrial anorak because only mentlers wear them as everyday jackets.

The address I wanted was in a new estate where everything looked a bit pokey.

Looking back, I don't know why I put a cartridge in the shotgun.

My revolver was always loaded and I had it in the back of my jeans.

But I never trusted the shotgun.

I had very few cartridges anyway.

Maybe I wanted to make some noise if this Mitchell guy knew how to take care of himself.

I'll never know, but it was one of the luckiest things I ever did.

I pulled on the balaclava and put the shotgun inside my jacket.

I thought I saw a curtain move upstairs but I wasn't sure.

I was ringing for about a minute when the door opened.

And there was a bloke in a balaclava.

He hit me in the face with a heavy cosh and grabbed my arm as I went for the shotgun.

He pulled me into the hall and kicked me on the back of the head.

I lay trying to get a grip on the radiator.

He slammed the door.

I heard a gun bolt and somebody said, "Don't move."

I froze.

My balaclava was pulled off and I was turned around.

My shotgun was on the hall table.

The man who'd grabbed me was standing in front of me and there was another one in overalls on the stairs holding an automatic rifle.

I knew this was out of my league and I was terrified.

I could see into the kitchen. Mitchell, who I was supposed to be scaring, was there with his wife and a little girl of about three or four.

Well, they were scared anyway.

The man on the stairs asked if Joe Murray had sent me and I immediately said yes, but that I was only there to threaten everybody.

The two men laughed at this and I laughed too.

I was hoping to make friends with them so they'd let me go. I know how stupid that sounds but these were professionals and they didn't give a shit.

The stairs man said they weren't going to kill me.

"Thanks," I said, and meant it.

He was all business and told me I was going to be shot in the legs, but they were afraid of ricochets so would I go out the back and lie on the grass?

I couldn't believe it.

Mitchell said something in the kitchen about not wanting them to do it there.

He was fat and baldy. The woman looked petrified.

The stairs man got annoyed and said, "What do you want us to fucking do? We can't drive around like this."

"What do I tell the guards?" said Mitchell.

The stairs man told him I couldn't go to the guards. They'd dump me miles away.

They argued about the noise gunshots would make.

The one in front of me suggested they use a sledgehammer on my legs.

They seemed to agree.

Mitchell was told to clear out for a few hours and take his missus with him.

And I was making up something you couldn't call a plan.

I didn't want to be a cripple for the rest of my life. I knew I'd have to pull the pistol from my pants and start shooting.

This was all pure panic.

The stairs man told Mitchell to go out the back way. But Mitchell said his keys were in the living room.

As he walked down the hall to the door beside me I grabbed the Webley and fired it straight ahead. I didn't bother taking aim. The shot hit the man in front of me in the hip and he collapsed on top of me, knocking the pistol on to the floor.

Then the stairs man started shooting.

He hit the living room doorjamb and the wall before getting Mitchell in the back. And then there was a clicking sound.

His rifle had jammed.

An empty cartridge was stuck in the breach and he was trying to release it by working the bolt back and forth.

I was on my knees and I pulled the shotgun from the hall table.

I saw the empty cartridge fly out of his gun and he accidentally fired a shot into the bannister.

I pointed the shotgun up the stairs, and without being sure I had cocked or even fired, it discharged a deafening shot.

The man jerked backwards up the stairs and landed sitting at the bathroom door.

I knew he was dead.

I hit the man in the hall over the head with the gun till he lay still, then I rolled him over and took my pistol.

Mitchell was still alive. He was shaking and losing a lot of blood.

His wife was trying to unlock the back door and keep her child in front of her.

I dragged her back and the child hung on.

I got them on to the floor and told them to shut up.

I slapped the woman on the neck. I meant to hit her face but I was shaking.

She quietened down and I told her I wasn't going to hurt them.

Then my legs went from under me.

My knees just buckled and I was on the floor beside them.

There was a phone on the worktop and I was trying to remember Joe Murray's number. When I got through, he wasn't in the bar. It took ages for them to get him.

He couldn't believe what had happened.

He told me to keep the woman and the kid there and not to do anything.

He was sending someone over.

The woman wasn't moving. She just held her kid, who seemed to be asleep.

I went through to the hall.

Mitchell was still breathing but it was a funny sound.

His face was pressed against the hinge of the half-opened door.

I thought there was blood coming out of his mouth.

Upstairs the dead man was still holding his rifle. He was sitting in a shower of pellet wounds.

Most of them were in his chest and shoulder but a few were in his neck and one or two in his face.

I took the magazine from his gun.

It was only a matter of time before the noise brought the guards to the house.

I decided to keep my options open.

The first sign of trouble I was getting out as fast as I could.

I took Mitchell's keys from the living room and went into the kitchen.

I asked Mrs. Mitchell if she was alright.

She just nodded and didn't look at me.

The kid looked drugged.

The kitchen had every modern appliance and for some reason that made me sad.

I was impatient. I wanted to get out.

I was watching Mitchell. He was breathing in shallow gasps.

The other man in the hall began to move a little bit. I told him to stay where he was. "What are you going to do?" he asked me. I told him some friends of mine were coming and he could explain his side of it to the guards while I was miles away having a pint.

Then he said it. "They're going to kill you."

Now whether he meant his buddies or mine, I didn't know. But I began to worry.

How the fuck did these guys know I'd be coming that morning? Vinnie Rourke didn't like me and Joe Murray would more than likely send him.

And I'd made a pig's mickey of this.

Mrs. Mitchell could identify me and sooner or later they'd trace me back to Murray. Mrs. Mitchell was in trouble and I was in trouble. One of us would have to go.

I was watching the street. Across the road a woman was standing in her porch.

She'd heard something, but she didn't seem to know what to do. She went back inside and a car pulled up. The driver kept it running. Vinnie Rourke and two others got out. One of them looked into my car and nodded at Rourke. He adjusted something in his jacket and walked towards the house.

I just knew.

I ran into the kitchen and shouted at Mrs. Mitchell to tell me where their car was.

It was in a garage out the back.

I heard the doorbell.

I ran down the garden and smashed the garage door open.

Mitchell's car was huge, a Rover, and the lane at the back of the house was narrow.

I heard shouting from the house and I thought about just legging it through the gardens. I stood in the garage and I couldn't decide what to do.

Then someone came out the back and called my name. It was Chris Breen, an old buddy of Vinnie Rourke's. He saw me.

He was holding a small pistol.

"Where are you going?" he said. "Come back."

I didn't move.

"We've got to get out of here," he said.

I stepped into the garden.

"What'll we do with the woman and the kid?" I asked him.

"Just come back in," he said.

I kept my hand on the butt of my revolver and pointed it at him through my jacket.

And we went back into the house.

Rourke's other mate, who I didn't know, had gagged Mrs. Mitchell and he was tying her hands behind her back.

The little girl was trying to cling to her mother. The man looked up from what he was doing and nodded at me.

Rourke was in the hall, strangling the man I'd wounded.

When he finished he stood up and looked at me. "This is a fucking mess," he said, "and I like the witnesses." He nodded at Mrs. Mitchell. Chris Breen was pointing his gun at me.

"What are you doing?" I said.

He smiled and shrugged at me.

I shot him through my pocket and ran backwards, slamming the kitchen door on Rourke.

The one I didn't know put his hands up.

Chris Breen was sitting on the floor.

I'd got him in the mouth. He was looking around like this was the first stuff he'd ever seen. I heard the front door as Rourke ran out to the car.

"Lean over the sink," I told Rourke's friend. "Put your head in the sink. If you move, I'll kill you," I told him.

I picked Mrs. Mitchell up and pushed her out the back. The kid clung to her leg.

I got them down to the garage and into the back of the car. Mrs. Mitchell lay across the back seat and the kid tumbled on to the floor.

The car was an automatic.

I had to keep my head to maneuver it into the lane.

I nudged it little by little and the lane opened up on to a road that ran around a green and then out to what looked like a main road.

I began to feel relieved, even jokey.

I asked Mrs. Mitchell if she wanted the radio on, and it seemed so ridiculous I started laughing. I was laughing and driving and I didn't know where I was going.

All I could think about was getting back to Greta and taking her away from Joe Murray. We could start again.

Then I heard sirens and knew we had to get out of the city.

We drove along Sundrive Road and Dolphin Road. Long roads with houses, garages, shops, undertakers, estate agents.

Eventually we hit the N4.

The sun was glinting in the rearview mirror. The eleven o'clock news had nothing yet. By lunchtime it'd be all over the place.

I pulled into a lay-by and shut the engine off. I leaned back and rubbed my face.

My hangover was coming back. I had hot flushes and shivers.

I got out and listened to the rain soaking into the ground, the odd car going past.

I bent over and got sick. The smell of whiskey and sugar made me retch again.

I knew I had to talk to Mrs. Mitchell, get her on my side. Buy us some time.

When I got myself together, I went back to the car. Mrs. Mitchell's head was against the door and the kid had climbed up on the seat beside her. She had a little blue dress on and one of her shoes was off.

Her hair was the same color as her mother's but her face was chubbier.

Mrs. Mitchell was very thin.

Her hands looked sore from the clothesline that tied them.

Her tracksuit bottoms were half off and I could have seen anything I wanted, but it just made me feel sick.

The kid was looking at me and Mrs. Mitchell was gasping for air.

There was snot all over her face and the rag around her mouth was soaking.

"Now Mrs. Mitchell," I said, "I'm going to talk to you and when you hear what I have to say, I'm going to untie you, do you understand me?" She nodded.

"When I untie you there's nowhere to run and I don't think you will if you listen to what I'm going to tell you. Can I trust you about these things?" She nodded again.

I sat in the driver's seat and began.

"Now listen, very soon the guards will be looking everywhere for us. There'll be roadblocks. I can't give you up because you can identify me. The men who came to your house were going to kill me and they were going to kill you.

"They'll have gotten out of there without leaving a whole lot of clues. They're old-time convicted rogues and they know what they're doing.

"I'm in no position to go to the police and neither are you.

"You knew what was going to happen to me and you didn't do anything."

She shook her head and made a noise.

I told her I'd take her gag off in a minute and she could say what she liked then. I told her I'd only come to scare her husband and that everything else was his fault, except for the bunch of cunts I worked for.

"Now I have no intention of hurting you," I told her. "It was the men your husband hired who shot him. It was an accident."

I made it clear I didn't want any of this but if we kept our heads and worked together we might live to tell the tale.

Joe Murray was sure to send Vinnie Rourke after us in case I blabbed to the guards as some sort of bargain.

He'd want Mrs. Mitchell too because she might link me to Murray.

Whoever the men who tried to break my legs were, if they were terrorists, their pals would be coming after us, and of course every guard in every shitty little fuckhole would have his eyes peeled.

She simply had to cooperate.

I asked her if she understood.

When she nodded, I leaned forward and took off the gag.

Then I pushed her up and undid her hands.

She sat up and held her kid.

"Thank you," she said.

I didn't feel like talking anymore.

"We've got to change this car," I said. "Next town, we're changing this car."

Then she said she didn't know what was going to happen at the house.

Mitchell's friends had come a few minutes before me. She didn't know who they were or what was going on.

I didn't say anything.

I just drove.

The news had been about a shooting and a possible kidnapping.

It was good being patchy. Right now the guards would be trying to figure out where Mrs. Mitchell might be without all the big search stuff.

She could be at the shops for all they knew.

Vinnie Rourke and the others must've gotten away. There were plenty of doctors Joe Murray knew who'd look after Chris Breen.

I reckoned Mr. Mitchell was dead.

I didn't say anything about it.

Mrs. Mitchell had her daughter on her lap. Things were peaceful.

I was beginning to see how lucky I'd been. Lucky or stupid.

I wondered which was worse, broken legs or being chased for killing someone.

Well I hadn't been caught, so maybe this was better.

I wanted to know what Greta would think.

This had to put me back at the center of her thoughts. I wanted to know if she was worried about me. Did she think I was a fucking idiot?

Then I thought about Joe Murray putting it up her arse.

I called her a fucking bitch and apologized to Mrs. Mitchell. I hadn't meant her. I hadn't meant her at all.

We drove into Kinnegad and I parked behind Jack's Bar, cum restaurant-B&B.

I asked Mrs. Mitchell if she wanted to get cleaned up.

She said okay. Then she asked me how I was for money.

I had about forty quid which wasn't going to get us very far.

She told me to take a map out of the glove compartment. There was a banklink card in the map. The name on it was Patrick Mitchell. "Do you know the number?" I stupidly asked her.

She just took it.

We left the car there.

This was her chance. If she wanted one.

All she had to do was grab someone or make a run for it. I didn't know if she had enough reasons to trust me. Or if she was afraid of me.

But we found a vending machine and she withdrew two hundred quid.

For someone who'd just seen her husband shot she was remarkably calm.

Maybe it's shock, I thought.

She picked the girl up in her lean arms and we went into Harry's, another bar down the street.

I told them to go and get cleaned up and not be too long about it.

It was twenty to one and some lunch people were sitting about. The more the better as far as I was concerned. I sank a pint and got another one. I knew I had to slow down. I didn't need the attention. I sat at the window and pretended to read a paper someone had left there.

A Bus Eireann bus had stopped across the street. The driver was helping a woman get her luggage from the side.

I ordered sandwiches and tea and soup.

Then I thought about the girl and got chips and ice cream. I drank a small one and it calmed me down. Took the edge off.

Mrs. Mitchell seemed hungry which I also thought was really odd.

The kid ate the ice cream then the chips.

Mrs. Mitchell was dipping her sandwiches in her soup. I got her a brandy and she drank it.

She called the kid Monkey. "Taste this, Monkey, wipe your hands." The kid was very quiet and well behaved. Mrs. Mitchell asked where we should go.

I had a friend who lived in Sligo—Jeff.

He owned an estate agents.

I thought he could give us somewhere to put our heads down for a few days, watch the news. See which way the guards jumped. How much they knew about her husband or if they linked the whole thing to Murray.

She didn't say whether she thought it was a good idea or not. Which was good enough for me. I told them to wait.

And I went out to look for an old-style Fiesta. These were cars I could start with very little hassle.

There was one outside the post office but there were too many people. I went the other way to where the road turns left at the end of the town.

There was a car park in front of some offices and a big factory.

I saw a woman get out of a 1981 Fiesta.

This was no bother.

I took out my keys and pretended to be wiping the windscreen of a Suzuki van.

When she was gone I went over and wrapped a stone in my jacket. I smashed the rear fly window on the driver's side.

When I reached in, the fucking thing was open already. That's the country.

I kicked the cover off the steering column and pulled the wires out of the ignition lock. I got it going in a couple of seconds and drove around in front of Harry's.

Mrs. Mitchell didn't make a fuss. She just came out and got in.

I was surprised. She got in the front.

I told them to be careful of the glass and then we U-turned and headed west again.

Mrs. Mitchell wanted to know what we'd do if we came across a roadblock.

We decided to pretend we were married.

"What's your name?" I asked the girl.

She didn't answer me.

"Niamh," said Mrs. Mitchell.

"Hello Niamh," I said.

"Hello," said Niamh.

We caught the headlines at half one.

Three bodies had been found in the house but hadn't been identified.

Mrs. Mitchell just looked out the window.

The traffic was heavy coming through Mullingar.

The rain came down in sheets.

I was relaxing. There wouldn't be roadblocks this far out.

I felt safe when we went through Longford without any hassle.

I was thinking about my friend, Jeff, who'd moved to Boyle a few years before any of this.

He sold houses and land in Sligo, Leitrim, Roscommon. We'd only seen each other once or twice since he'd moved.

I'd stayed with him in a house no one was buying, on the Shannon.

Greta had come and we drank and went out in a boat, all that sort of stuff.

Jeff had a wife and four kids, but he was very laid back. I trusted him and I hoped he could sort us out.

He knew what I did for a living and one time I'd helped him out.

A local councillor called Burke had hinted that Jeff would have to pay what he called an "administration fee" of five grand for planning permission for two bungalows Jeff was building for some people in Dublin.

Jeff said this was bollocks and told the councillor to fuck off.

A couple of nights later while Jeff was having a piss in the pub, someone punched him on the back of the head.

He broke a front tooth on the tiling.

He got a few kicks and someone told him to get his responsibility as a citizen together. And all that tat.

This told him that Burke must have been behind it.

He phoned me in Dublin.

He was scared. He wanted Burke off his back but didn't want to know the details.

I drove to Boyle on a Tuesday afternoon.

Burke spent his afternoons in a pub called the Riverside. He drank with men who worked for him. Delivering peat briquettes.

They watched the telly for racing results.

Burke never spoke to anyone unless they spoke to him.

I watched him mill five or six pints and when I saw him get ready to go I slipped out in front of him.

I followed him home. He drove a Mercedes.

He lived across from his farm which was a series of fields along a bend in the river. It was a nice spot.

I sat and waited, enjoying the peace and quiet. I wanted to make sure he was alone. He had no children. His wife left the house around five. She was a nurse.

A few minutes later, Burke came out with wellies and a walking stick.

He went down to the river and looked at the bank. There was some flooding.

I got out and waved at him.

He turned and waved back.

I walked towards him with a friendly smile.

He gripped his stick a little tighter and watched me carefully. He was much bigger than me and I knew I'd have to fuck him up very quickly.

When I was about fifteen feet away from him, I started to say, "I wonder if you could tell me where I might find a place called . . ."

And I kicked the shit out of him.

I kicked him as he tried to run away.

I kicked him on the ground and I hit him with his stick until I was exhausted.

Then I picked him up and punched and dragged him back up to his house.

He collapsed on the driveway but I kicked his arse and got him inside.

"Where's the kitchen?" I asked him.

"I don't have any money here," he said.

I told him to shut up.

I didn't want to tell him Jeff had sent me in case Burke's friends did something to him.

I wanted to fuck him up generally so that he'd be too scared to do anything to anybody. And I wanted him in the kitchen because that's where people keep their knives.

Mrs. Mitchell wanted to use the toilet so we stopped in Carrick on Shannon.

The news had that one of the dead men had been identified as Dublin businessman, Patrick Mitchell.

The gardai were interviewing witnesses at the scene.

A woman had seen three men come out of the house and one of them was hurt. I knew that was Chris Breen.

Two of the men had gone in Vinnie Rourke's car and another had taken mine.

They were afraid of my car being linked to Joe Murray. This wasn't working out so bad. There were no definite leads.

When Mrs. Mitchell and Niamh came back I said, "Listen, if there's anyone you want to call and say you're okay, I think you should, but just don't tell them where you are yet."

She just nodded.

I asked her if she was alright.

I was curious at how calm she was.

"Are you in shock?" I said.

She asked me what I meant.

I said I didn't know and she laughed.

I was beginning to think Mrs. Mitchell was a bit of a loolah.

We drove over a bridge and a sign said Boyle, twelve miles.

"My friend, Jeff," I was telling her, "always has empty houses, secluded, we can probably stay somewhere like that for a day or two and work things out. Is that okay?"

"Yes," she said. As if she was annoyed at me. Then Niamh said something about a tree and we smiled.

I was watching the road and thinking about what people were like.

I was tired. There was a house right beside the road. I wanted to live there so I could pull in, sit by the fire and have a few drinks. Eat my dinner and go to bed and in bed, my pretty wife would tell me she wasn't my judge and I'd sleep and sleep and dream until the next thing I'd do, which would be an interesting thing.

And no one would bother me.

The day was dark and the rain becoming torrential when we got to Boyle.

Mrs. Mitchell waited in the car.

I went over to Jeff's offices beside the memorial and I saw him through the door.

He was talking to a woman who was typing at a computer.

I looked around and went in.

"Jesus," said Jeff.

I smiled and asked him if he had a minute.

"Come on," he said, and we went into his office.

"I'm in trouble," I told him.

"I'm going to be straight with you. I've killed someone and I need somewhere to go."

"Is this the thing on the radio?" he said.

"It's not my fault," I told him.

"They're looking for a woman and a kid."

He was smarter than he looked.

"It's not a kidnap," I told him. "They're in the car." I told him what had happened.

He sat down and didn't look well for a few minutes and then he said, "Come on."

I followed him out. He asked his secretary for some keys.

"Wait till you see this place," he said.

We went out into the rain.

"Get them," said Jeff. "We'll take my car and dump that one later."

And as I ran across to the Fiesta, he shouted, "It's nice to see you." I swung around and we were laughing.

I told Mrs. Mitchell we'd been sorted out.

Niamh had been sick.

"That's okay, Niamh," I said. "It's not our car."

Jeff pulled alongside and Mrs. Mitchell took Niamh into the back.

I introduced everyone.

Jeff said, "How are you Niamh, chicken, a bit car sick?"

"She's alright now," said Mrs. Mitchell.

"And how are you?" said Jeff.

"I'm okay," she said.

Then Jeff said, "It's over now, I promise you'll all be safe."

Mrs. Mitchell said this was the worst rain she'd ever seen, and Jeff asked us if it was raining in Dublin.

I wondered if I was in a car full of fucking loopers.

We drove for about ten miles with the wipers on full tilt.

Jeff was telling us a story about a time his car was stuck in the mud after he'd been drinking at some festival in Galway.

It was one of those stories where everyone ends up covered in mud, pushing the wrong car into a lake.

I closed my eyes and listened to Jeff.

And I could feel Niamh's breath in my ear as she stood between the seats.

I wondered if things were getting better or if Jeff was just one of those people.

"And here we are," he said.

We turned through a pair of huge gates and drove up a tree-lined avenue.

And in a wide hollow was a house as big as the GPO.

"Be it ever so humble," said Jeff.

"Look where we're going to stay, Niamh," said Mrs. Mitchell.

Jeff was grinning to save his life.

We went in through high narrow doors.

We were in a tiled hallway.

The door straight ahead led to a similar back hall and we could see a huge garden which sloped down to the Shannon where it was wide and islands stretched across to a newly planted forest.

We walked around looking for ghosts.

Jeff was talking to us.

But I wasn't listening. I was too busy smelling the air.

The rooms were empty and recently refloored.

The boards gave off an unexpected warmth.

The rain hammered off the windows.

I stood in the darkening ballroom.

Jeff took Mrs. Mitchell with Niamh in her arms up to the next floor.

I heard him tell her how surprisingly cheap a place like this was.

I sat with my back to the wall and put my revolver on my lap.

I closed my eyes and listened to the rain and the wind.

I was dreaming about the heart of the countryside beating.

I was in the veins like a sickness and Greta's hands were in my clean hair and we lay just beneath the clouds wondering when the storm would end.

I woke to sunshine blazing across the floor. I was wrapped in a quilt and soft little hands were on my face. Niamh ran across to the windows in her bare feet.

I heard voices. Laughing. Children shouting. My revolver was pressing against my shoulderblade.

I sat up. It was eleven o'clock.

Jeff came in and said, "You're alive." Fucking comedian.

He had a flask.

He sat down beside me and I drank a cup of coffee.

He told me he had brought his wife, Marie, and the kids over. Marie and Mrs. Mitchell were organizing a picnic. This was blowing my mind.

I wanted to know if we were safe.

"I think so," he said.

He showed me the papers.

People seemed to think it was some sort of fucked-up IRA thing, which suited me fine.

The guards were appealing for information about the cars.

They didn't have any registrations.

They found Mitchell's car in Kinnegad, and they were looking for the Fiesta.

Nobody had seen us yet.

Jeff had it stashed in the garage of a house he was selling which didn't get many viewers.

As long as nothing linked it to me or Murray no one would find us up here in Leitrim, which is where we turned out to be.

Jeff gave me clean clothes and razors and stuff. I showered upstairs in an en-suite bathroom.

Out the window I could see Mrs. Mitchell and Marie organizing blankets on the lawn.

Everything was on a huge plastic sheet.

Jeff was playing with the kids.

He picked Niamh up and swung her around, chasing the others with her in his arms.

She was in hysterics.

On the blankets Jeff's baby was lying on her belly, rolling onto her back.

I went down.

Marie kissed me and gave me a long hug.

Mrs. Mitchell smiled at me.

I sat down and played with the baby.

She squeezed my fingers tightly, even though she was tiny.

I liked the pressure.

There were sandwiches, meat, salad, cake, wine, beer and coffee all on paper plates spread over the blankets.

I smoked one of Marie's Marlboro's and had a beer.

I held the baby on my lap and we all laughed at her.

Mrs. Mitchell sat beside me and drank Piât D'Or from a paper cup.

She said she hadn't seen Niamh have so much fun in ages.

"They're great kids," I said.

Marie took the baby from me to change her nappy. Jeff was rounding up the children.

I asked Mrs. Mitchell if she'd seen the papers. She said she had and then became upset. I tried to comfort her, but she pulled away from me and said, "Look, you're not my friend, okay?"

I nodded.

We didn't say anything for a minute.

Then she said, "Sorry."

And I said, "No."

She said she'd made a call.

"To who?" I asked her.

But Marie came back, shouting, "Come on, everybody."

The kids stuffed themselves.

I was starving too.

I must've ate about a loaf of seafood sandwiches which were Marie's thing.

I drank a few beers, but I really wanted to get Mrs. Mitchell on her own and ask her who the fuck she'd called.

So I asked her to come for a walk.

We went down to the river.

The baby was crying.

"Who did you ring?" I asked her.

She sat on a rock and put her feet in the water.

"Oh that's freezing," she said. "I thought it'd be warmer."

I smacked the back of her head and grabbed her hair.

I told her that if she fucked me around, I'd break every bone in her body.

I'd really lost my temper.

She didn't shout. She didn't make a sound.

I let her go and she said, "I rang Niamh's father, alright?"

I wanted to know what she was talking about.

"Patrick Mitchell wasn't her father," she said. "I had been seeing someone."

She gave me a story about some teenage sweetheart coming back into her life a year or two after she'd married Mitchell.

She wouldn't sleep with Mitchell and he was going bananas. He was going to move them all to England which is why he was trying to sort the Joe Murray thing out.

But there was no way she was going.

She wanted to be with this man.

But he was a journalist who traveled around a lot and he wasn't ready to settle down and support them.

That's why she was still with Mitchell when he died.

Like so many fucking things.

She needed a roof over her head.

So she'd rung this man in Paris saying what had happened, but that she was safe.

She hadn't told him where she was but he was coming to Ireland.

"You have to believe me," she said.

I did believe her.

For one thing, it seemed to explain her less than widowly grief.

"You make me sick," I said. And walked off. She chased me and punched my back.

"What do you mean?" she shouted.

But I knew I hadn't meant her.

I was sorry I'd said it.

She became upset again and this time when I put my arm around her, she cried into my chest.

And I was thinking about Joe Murray on top of Greta.

I told her I was sure it would work out.

"Come on Mrs. Mitchell," I said, "let's have a drink."

She laughed at me calling her Mrs. Mitchell and said her name was Anna.

I told her I was sorry for all the shit that had happened. But I was trying to feel sorry and I don't think I really did.

Not that I was glad. I don't mean that at all.

She seemed to cheer up a little bit then and we spent the rest of the afternoon drinking and watching the children.

The baby fell asleep in my arms.

Jeff went down and swam. The kids jumped around on the shore and he splashed them.

The rest of us smoked and chatted occasionally.

At dusk it began to get a bit chilly.

We went inside and sat in the ballroom.

The children were tired and it was time for Jeff to bring his family home.

Marie was saying good-bye to Mrs. Mitchell.

I wondered if I should ring Joe Murray.

But Jeff said he'd be back in the morning and we could decide what to do then.

Mrs. Mitchell had slept upstairs the night before but she moved her stuff down beside mine.

When Jeff was gone she laid Niamh down in the quilt and we spoke quietly for a while.

Her boyfriend was a freelance writer and she seemed to love him very much. He knew he was Niamh's father, but he'd only seen her three times.

Mr. Mitchell had thought Niamh was his.

She had been conceived during a two-week daily sex session at the Mitchell's house while he was at work.

I felt sorry for the poor bastard.

Mrs. Mitchell hoped to get out of the country without being involved in any investigation.

We joked for a while about what color she should dye her hair to avoid being recognized. She wanted to know what I was going to do. I didn't know. I told her I hadn't any commitments or ties.

I sort of wanted to talk about Greta but I didn't know where to begin.

We settled down for the night.

I could feel them lying beside me and when I listened to them breathing it felt like my soul was being bleached.

I woke to the sound of glass breaking.

"What is it?" I heard Mrs. Mitchell say.

It was pitch dark.

I took my pistol and told her to stay where she was.

I made my way to the front door.

It was open and the breeze filled the hall.

I couldn't see anyone.

I moved my way back toward the ballroom, feeling for a light switch.

"Mrs. Mitchell?" I whispered.

A torch went on and something bounced off my head.

I was very groggy.

I could see that dawn was coming and that there were people in the room.

My hands were cuffed behind me and I had no clothes on.

I was sitting on the floor.

I passed out again.

Then I was slapped.

This time it was brighter.

Vinnie Rourke's friend, Seamus Parker was slapping me.

"Get your fucking hands off me," I said.

Someone kicked me in the back. I collapsed and I couldn't move.

The feeling came back gradually and I wished it wouldn't.

"Get him up," someone said.

I was dragged to my feet by Seamus Parker and someone else I didn't know.

Vinnie Rourke stood in front of me and quick as he could, he gave me three digs, two in the stomach and one in the face.

He did it so fast I knew he was showing off.

I took a step backwards but they held me steady.

"Where's Joe Murray?" I asked.

They all started digging me.

I was surprised how weak their punches were.

Maybe it was they were up all night.

I was getting worried about Mrs. Mitchell and Niamh. But I didn't want to say anything.

I didn't want to draw attention to them.

I wanted them to be forgotten.

Vinnie Rourke grabbed my bollocks and gave them a good wrench.

It was agony, but it was sort of funny.

I asked him if he was enjoying himself.

He got a bit annoyed.

I said I never knew he was a poof.

That did the job. He let go and told me he'd show me who was a poof.

He kicked my legs so hard I was leaping in Seamus Parker's arms.

Then I was on the floor.

I knew he'd break my neck if he kept kicking me. I was passing out.

I saw Greta and Mrs. Mitchell leading me up some stairs in newly painted flats beside a river. There was a war and they were looking after me.

Then I was drenched on the floor.

Vinnie Rourke had poured a bucket of water over me.

My left eye was closing.

I could just see Joe Murray sitting on a chair above me.

Nobody said anything.

I smiled at him and he looked away.

Then he asked me what I thought I was playing at.

I tried to speak and something fell out of my mouth.

I ran my tongue along the gaps in my teeth.

"For fuck's sake," said Murray.

I managed to say "How . . . ?"

"How did we find you?" he said. "Don't be dense. Greta knew where you'd go. You see," he said, "she loves me so she told me. How does that make you feel?"

I was disappointed, but something cheered me up. And it was something I knew about and Joe Murray didn't. Greta didn't love anybody. He didn't know her at all.

"What are you grinning at?" he said. "You little bastard. We looked after your friend. We looked after that fucker."

I knew he must have found out where we were from Jeff. But Jeff wouldn't have told him simply because he was asked nicely.

"It was like the towering fucking inferno," he said.

I thought he might be bluffing but I wasn't very hopeful that Jeff and his family were still alive.

I was waiting for him to get on with it and shoot me.

I wondered whose fault this was.

"And I suppose you want to know about flat-chest Mitchell and the sprog?" said Murray. And the way he said it told me everything.

When I was out cold, they'd had a party.

Maybe that dream I'd had of her when I was getting that kicking was her soul and she had met me while things were happening to her body. I still like to think that.

Murray was talking.

"Greta did us a favor telling me where you were, and we're going to do something for her. She asked us to let you live."

I couldn't believe it. She had been thinking about me. She wanted me to be alive.

He went on.

"We've worked something out. In a few hours you'll be arrested here. There'll be evidence the Mitchells were here, but not enough to completely fuck you. Keep your mouth shut, make something up and you'll get accessory, five to ten years we reckon."

He got up and signaled the others to go.

Then he said, "Mention me or anybody and we'll kill you. I'm only doing this for Greta. She says I can trust you. And I have to trust her. Don't I? I mean, I'm not young anymore. I have to make a commitment."

I motioned to him with my head and he leaned over me.

"Just don't put it in her arse," I said.

I don't know if he heard me or not.

He just got up and left.

I lay there throbbing from the kicks and I thought my heart would burst.

Sure enough towards afternoon the guards came.

I was taken to hospital and I wouldn't answer any questions.

I turned off in every interrogation.

I just thought about Greta.

I was wondering what she was doing at the precise moment I was thinking about her.

Funny, I always imagined her having a bath.

Eventually I confessed to a kidnapping.

But I said I was only the driver.

I didn't know that Mitchell had been killed and I was waiting for a ransom for us to release Mrs. Mitchell.

The other kidnappers had double-crossed me and beat me. I didn't know their real names. I thought they were English.

The guards saw this for the rubbish it was, but it was all they had.

They'd found me tied up and in bits. They knew I couldn't have done that to myself, and although they linked me to Jeff, whoever had done the arson job on his house had made it look accidental enough.

My army record was good, I'd never been arrested before.

Mrs. Mitchell and Niamh were never found.

No bodies, no murder charge.

At my trial I think everyone thought I was some sort of idiot.

But fuck that. I got ten years.

I didn't think very much for the next few weeks.

I just went along day by day.

I felt sad all of the time.

But I'm not sure what I felt sad about.

And I know how stupid that sounds.

Then the sad feeling went and I just thought about Greta.

I wanted to kill Joe Murray and Vinnie Rourke.

It was the only reason I wanted to get out.

And after that I didn't really feel anything.

Sometimes I woke up thinking Niamh's hands were on my face and I would wish that everyone was still alive. But these were more feelings than thoughts.

They ran through me and they were spilt milk.

I knew nothing good could come out of what had happened because of everybody's stupidity.

Then one day someone was put in my cell with me.

His name was Tom Vander.

He was twenty, a burglar.

We didn't speak much to begin with, which isn't to say we weren't friendly.

He didn't make many friends and pretty much stayed on his own.

Then one evening we just sort of got talking.

He had started breaking into houses around where he lived, in Clontarf, about a year before.

He liked the feeling of being in someone else's house with all their private things.

Sometimes, he'd even take a bath.

I thought this was very funny.

He never stole much. Just cash, if he found it, but he never looked very hard.

The odd time he'd watch their videos or look through their books.

He might sound a bit spacey, but he was alright. He was a good laugh.

We never bothered each other if one of us wasn't in a talky mood.

We were happy enough reading or just listening to tapes.

One night I told him all about Mrs. Mitchell and Niamh and everything that had happened.

He didn't say anything about it and I was glad he didn't. He just knew it was something you couldn't say anything about.

I told him about Greta and he told me about his girlfriends and how he'd had sex up a tree one time.

That night I heard him wanking in the bunk above me and I wanked too.

We wanked a lot after that. We knew when either of us were doing it and we made up filthy stories while we did it.

This usually ended in hysterics.

Then one blazing summer's day, Tom was released.

I knew he was getting out but I hadn't thought about it much. He was delighted and I was too. But then I felt crap because one day he was there and the next he wasn't and I couldn't talk to him anymore.

He went to England.

He wrote for a while and then he got engaged and didn't write after that.

My own company wasn't good enough for me anymore.

And it wasn't that I wanted to be entertained or anything, I wanted to make someone else happy.

I wanted to be there when they needed me.

I don't live in Ireland anymore.

I drink too much and I hardly go out.

I sometimes wonder about the type of person I am, but not for long.

I'm no good.

Sometimes when the clouds are low and I look out the window with one eye on the pillow I still think about Mrs. Mitchell and Niamh and Jeff's family.

And I think about Greta and the time I saw her last year.

It was a filthy wet day and she got out of a big car with a man twice her age.

I thought about walking up to her but I was trying to get out of the rain.

End of Play

RUM AND
VODKA

For The Fly by Nights

Rum and Vodka was first performed at University College Dublin on November 27, 1992. It was performed by Stephen Walshe and directed by Conor McPherson.

It was subsequently performed at the City Arts Centre, Dublin, on August 30, 1994, by Fly by Night Theatre Company. It was performed by Jason Byrne and directed by Colin O'Connor

PART ONE

I think my overall fucked-upness is my impatience.

I could never wait for anything to be over.

And I think that's the sign of an inquiring mind.

I don't want to do the investigations, I just want the answers.

And I reckon that because of that I'm a bit of a pessimist.

Because I never got any.

And that can lead to a lack of social graces.

I always feel that wherever I go, people look at me with a squinty face as if to say, "Now, just who the fuck are you?"

I think I hate the human race.

And I think they know it.

I often think the world gets together behind my back while I'm on the jacks or in bed and makes hasty decisions about new ways to get me to leave the planet.

They leave the meeting laughing.

Now, that's got to be the king of conspiracy theories.

But I know it's not true.

I suppose my impatience is due to my embarrassment a lot.

Maybe I don't like myself too much.

I hate looking back at things I've done.

So I'm always doing something new.

That means that my memories are like being different people.

But that's all a load of shit.

What I really want to tell you about is what's happened to me over the last three days.

I'm twenty-four going twenty-five.

I live on a new, well fairly new, estate in Raheny.

I'm married.

I have two young girls.

Until a couple of days ago I worked for the voting registration department of the corporation on Wellington Quay.

I'd been working there since I got married.

When I was twenty.

You might think that's quite young for someone to get married these days.

And I probably agree with you.

But em . . .

I had been going out with a girl since I was eighteen.
We had been going out for two years.

And I mean, you're twenty.

What the fuck do you know? I mean, I was still trying the world for size.

Do you understand me? I was arsing about.

You know? I was messing.

With other girls.

I don't think I ever meant it to happen.

It usually happened when I had too much to drink.

But, ah . . . I was at this party one night and I ended up half comatose in the back garden.

And this girl, friend of a friend, decided she was going to look after me.

While I got sick in her shoe.

She stayed with me all night.

And I was grateful and I thought I felt something for her, and as the night wore on and everyone went home it was mostly horny.

I'm not going into the sordid details.

My life's one big sordid detail.

But we ended up being intimate.

On a number of occasions that night.

And I ended up seeing her for, well, whatever reasons after that.

And all the while I was still going out with my girlfriend and this other girl, the party girl, knew I was. Alright?

And then when the chewing gum lost its taste I stopped seeing her and decided to be faithful again.

For, well, forever.

But then I got a phone call from the party girl.

She was having a baby.

And now she's my wife.

You have to understand I didn't marry her for religious or moral . . . I mean, we didn't have to get married at all.

But as more and more people found out . . .

My mum and dad were furious.

My friends thought I was a fucking fool because they liked my girlfriend.

And my girlfriend.

Well I think it's the worst thing that ever happened to her in her life.

And . . . I have nothing else to say about that except that sometimes I . . . miss her.

So anyway.

There I was.

Lowest of the low, with no one really to turn to except this pregnant girl.

And she was the only one who didn't criticize me.

We got on well enough and the more shit I got off other people the more I found comfort with her.

I ended up saying, "Fuck you, everybody!"

Got a job, hundred and eighty quid a week, got a mortgage and figured my life finally had some direction.

And I got down to it.

I was the real nine to five animal.

And it was alright.

I spent the next two years getting on with making money, getting my wife pregnant again and drinking at the weekends.

The thrill of having your own house.

I could do what I liked.

I was a pretty good family man.

I remembered birthdays and I was Santa.

And the freedom.

I was always waiting for a knock at the door and a slap. But it wasn't going to come. I was grown-up. I was allowed.

If I wanted to I could drink till three o'clock, watch videos till dawn, fuck my missus.

I mean, she was always there.

And that's one thing about that marriage.

Maybe there's never been too much . . . I don't know, but that's always been more than made-up for in the bedroom.

Even from the outset.

We were married in a registry office.

There was very little ceremony.

But we spent our honeymoon in the house we were buying.

In Raheny.

And even though she was quite pregnant we got up to some of the weirdest stuff.

She's always been insatiable.

She often wakes me up with a cup of coffee which is like just an excuse.

She wants me there and then.

Even when she was huge with the baby she'd insist on doing it standing up with me behind her.

The complaints department weren't exactly run off their feet.

The kids came in a year of each other so we really had two babies in the house for a while.

I've never been gone on kids but I got a real kick out of these girls.

I know it's cruel, but I used to laugh at them trying to walk, falling on their arses or walking into chairs.

I thought that was very funny.

But as they got older I sort of felt like I was just playing at being Mr. Daddy.

And it all got a bit unreal. A bit hard to believe.

I still felt eighteen or sixteen.

And it came as quite a shock when I realized that this was as good as things were going to get.

I found myself ticking off the minutes at work, skiving in and out of flexi-time, and, most importantly, drinking a lot.

This year especially it's got to the stage where I'm getting pissed every day.

The only days I don't drink are the ones where I'm too sick to move.

And it's this that really leads me on to the last three days.

Maria, my wife, and I've been fighting a lot recently.

She's been giving out about the money I'm spending, saving nothing, not coming in till one or two every morning.

Thing is, on top of everything, I'm an awful stupid bastard with money.

I don't drive and I jump in and out of taxis like there's no tomorrow.

I know it's ridiculous, but I don't know . . .

I'm just lazy . . .

I'm a thick fucker.

I tried cycling into work for a while.

I haven't cycled in years and Maria said it would keep me in shape as well as cutting down on expenses.

It worked for about three days.

I left the bike in the car park under work, but that meant it got locked in after six.

If I wanted to go for a few jars I'd have to lock it on the street somewhere.

I locked it to the railings of a house on Wellington Quay but then I decided to lock it inside the railings to make it harder to nick.

It worked because it was still there at half twelve that night.

Trouble was . . . my judgment was impaired.

When I unlocked it, it fell right down into the basement.

All the lights in the house went on.

I ran down Wellington Quay because sometimes I'm shy.

I had no money for a taxi and I started walking, thinking I'd get the bike back in the morning.

I must have gotten some fright though, because only when I was half way up North Strand did I realize I was holding half a U-lock.

I think I'd have to say that my drinking or habitual drinking is due to two of the men I work with.

Phil Comesky and Declan Short.

They live together in a house in Killester which is the most disgraceful kip I've ever seen.

There's leftovers and remains of about a thousand take-aways, bottles, cans, socks, the place stinks.

It's a mixture of rotting and deodorant. They must spray the air.

I've ended up there hundreds of nights.

They drink, I mean drink, get drunk every day. They smoke about forty each as well.

They're both odd in their own ways.

Declan's got this girlfriend he's been going out with for about ten years.

They always fight. But you should see her drink. Pints. That's what keeps their flame aglow.

They fall around in each others' arms at closing time. Then they get two naggins. Vodka for him, Jameson or Powers for her, as long as it's Irish.

Every day. I'm serious.

Declan doesn't even have a beer belly.

He's one of those people who can drink a keg of Guinness, get four hours' sleep, and still look like he runs a health food shop.

I sometimes think that he'll be eating his breakfast one morning and it'll catch up with him. He'll disintegrate in seconds.

His girlfriend is a state though.

She looks like her mother shat her.

And that's pure drink.

Phil's the real spacer though.

He's been in and out of mental homes up till a few years ago.

When he was fourteen a boy on his road was killed when he was hit by a car.

It was a big tragedy at the time.

Big turnout at the funeral.

The boy who'd been killed had a girlfriend. They had been going out for about three weeks.

I mean. At that age.

She threw a letter into the grave when the coffin was being lowered.

And . . . she was young. She got over it.

She grew up.

Now, when Phil was twenty, no one knows why, because he didn't even know the girl, he dug up the grave and got this letter out.

He broke into the girl's house at three o' clock in the morning, sat on her bed, and read it to her.

Nearly drove her mad.

I mean. That's real bonkers for you.

Anyway.

Last Friday lunchtime we were out having a drink.

We sank four pints each and I knew the weekend was going to be bananas.

I had been so depressed all week that to get paid meant get pissed.

Trouble was I was already hungover from the night before and my body was staging a coup.

I was finding it difficult to keep anything down.

All I wanted was to put my head on the desk and die.

I would have knocked off early saying I was sick, but there was some fuck-up with the checks and no one was getting paid till four.

So I sat there sleepy and sick.

Bored stupid, wondering how I was going to get through the afternoon.

And everything went haywire.

Even now it's a blur.

Eamon Meaney, our arsehead of an office manager, came over to my desk in his Farah slacks and Clarke's shoes.

He used to be a national school teacher but he threw a tantrum one day and got fired. He was completely bald and thought he was gorgeous.

He had two queries with my work, and while I tried to dig myself out of a hole full of shit, I saw his expression change.

"Have you been drinking?" he asked me.

"I had a glass of wine with my lunch," I slurred.

I must have smelled like a brewery, because he asked me just who I thought I was, getting drunk on taxpayers' time and money.

I said I didn't know.

He told me to get into his office and walked off.

And I sat there.

Looking at the buildings on Batchelor's Walk, all falling down and filthy.

I saw the last name I had typed on my Apple Mac, Helen Falconer.

What a name.

Her ancestors must have been falconers.

Wow, I thought.

Meaney shouted across the room at me to hurry up.

Everyone looked at me.

People from every county.

I went red from my shoulders to my scalp and . . . I picked up my terminal, and I swung it out the window.

It sailed down two flights and right through the windscreen, and I didn't mean this, of Eamon Meaney's car.

Okay, I had a choice.

I could pretend to have a nervous breakdown and beg everyone's pity, or I could brazen it out.

"Do you have any idea how long I've wanted to do that for?" I said.

They stared at me.

Meaney took a step backwards.

I picked up my jacket and strode out of the office.

As I went down the stairs I heard the door slam. I hadn't meant it but I was glad it did.

The day was overcast and people moved about on the street.

I went straight to the Norseman.

A pint and a short.

Never drank so fast.

Same again.

People in the pub.

Friday lunchtimers taking the afternoon off. Justified.
They'd done their work.

And I felt so stupid and sick and guilty and angry and . . . low.

I wasn't very happy.

But I was glad of a drink.

It took the edge off my worries.

Brought out my self-reliance.

If things are going well it helps you congratulate yourself.

If you're in the shitter it gives you all the righteous indigna-
tion of an innocent victim.

And by five o'clock I felt both.

At six Phil and Declan came in.

I was quite a sensation.

By seven we were discussing my future plans.

Fuck, the three of us'd go into business together.

We were going to be gardeners.

Out in nature and stuff.

No more fluorescent lights or instant coffee.

And oh yeah, no more drinking.

It was time to take our lives by the scruff said Phil and he
got change for the cigarette machine.

We were mates said Declan.

I told the lads I loved them.

I told them I'd wanted to say that for a long time.

We all embraced and I went for a piss.

By ten the place was jammed.

None of us were talking much.

Just drinking.

I thought I was getting a temperature.

The floor swayed and I puked on the carpet.

We moved away from that spot and since the barmen hadn't seen, we got another one in.

By eleven I was nearly asleep.

The whole day felt like something that had happened to someone else.

I put my head in my hands and cried.

I cried until my eyes stung, till my gums felt swollen, till I couldn't lick my lips.

Then it was time to go.

Phil and Declan were arguing about economics. The argument went something like, "Fuck you." "No fuck you." "That's bollocks." "You're a cunt." "Me?"

Like that. Like every fucking night.

Declan bought a bottle from behind the bar and we headed for the lads' house.

We had to stop the taxi for me to be sick and while I did, Phil ran up the road and got a Chinese.

Declan's girlfriend was back at the house with some friend of hers from Denmark.

I tried some whiskey but my throat was raw and I nearly got sick again.

Phil vanished upstairs with Miss Denmark and Declan and Siobhan crashed out on the couch.

I went outside. It was nearly two.

I walked along the Howth road to Raheny.

I turned left up Station Road and into my estate.

We live in at the back, in a cul-de-sac.

I went in quietly and took four paracetamol.

The lights were all out upstairs.

I undressed in the dark.

I was too tired to look for pajamas.

I just slipped under the quilt and stayed as far over my side as possible.

I curled in a ball and shivered.

Maria moved close and held me.

I knew I was going to break her heart.

I'd always known it.

I wished I could wake her up and talk but I was too tired to think.

And then the curse of any tender moment, an erection.

I suddenly wanted her more than ever.

And drink'll do that to you.

And all this . . . aggression.

This is my house.

I'm in bed with my wife.

And I'm going to fuck her now.

I rolled over and felt her tits.

She was warm and soft.

I pulled the front of her nightie up and felt between her legs.

She was fast asleep.

I waited till she was ready, then I held myself above her like I was going to do press-ups, and I slid inside her.

Suddenly it was bright.

It was morning.

The kids were shouting out the back.

I had a massive headache.

Like something was bursting out of my head.

My throat was sore and my mouth was so dry my tongue grated along the roof of my mouth when I unstuck it from my teeth.

And then I remembered . . .

Everything came flooding back and my stomach leapt.

This was very serious.

I could go to jail.

I needed a drink.

Fuck. Had I pulled out of Maria? Had she woken up to find me stuck up her? Did she have to push me off with disgust? I could hear her in the kitchen.

What was I going to say? I wanted to crawl under the quilt and hide like a kid.

I got up.

My clothes stank of smoke.

I put on Maria's dressing gown and went down to the kitchen.

"Hi, hi."

"You were late"

". . . Yeah."

She didn't seem any more annoyed than usual.

I must have pulled out.

I mean, that's pretty close to rape.

She'd have done her nut.

The kids saw me. "Daddy, Daddy."

I didn't know which was worse my headache or my guilt.

I couldn't take any tablets because Maria would start on at me about drinking.

I didn't want that.

What I was really worried about was how I was going to tell her I didn't think I had a job anymore.

I ate a greasy fried egg I knew wasn't going to stay down, went upstairs, turned on the shower and puked into the toilet.

The shower was cold.

The immersion hadn't been on and I couldn't get a lather from the soap.

You see, this was a bit of a crisis because every Saturday we do the big shop.

We go down to Crazy Prices in Kilbarrack.

I knew I had about twenty-five quid in my jacket, but the messages usually come to about forty-five/fifty.

I was in trouble.

There was no way of not facing the music.

I had to tell her I'd no check.

But she was busy when I got dressed.

Getting the buggy ready, I don't know.

I was so tired.

I sat in the living room and closed my eyes.

I had no idea how to go about this.

Then we were up and out.

Walking down the street.

Carol in my arms.

Niamh in the buggy.

Maria saying hello to people.

Up Raheny Hill.

Carol's hair on my face.

Into the car park.

It was starting to drizzle.

We got a trolley, Maria's list, and we were shopping.

I was forming mad plans.

I'm on a diet, I don't need food.

Let's have a severe economy drive.

But she'd know something was up.

And it was.

Something was up.

The trolley was filling up.

Maria was saying, "Pampers, Pampers, toilet roll."

I was pushing the trolley.

"Maria . . ."

"Yogurt, cheese . . ."

"Maria . . ."

"Mm?"

"Maria, I just remembered.

"I never cashed the check, we got them late and I . . ."

"What . . . ?"

"I think I've lost my job."

"What are you saying? Put that down Carol."

"I threw my terminal out the window.

"I'm so sorry."

Maria went white.

She was puzzled.

She wanted this to be a joke but she knew it wasn't. And there was nothing I could do.

"I'm sorry."

She hit me across the eye with a can of tuna.

I think I blacked out.

I tumbled backwards into a freezer with Bird's Eye fishfingers and pizzas and shit.

I could hear Maria screaming and she was thumping my legs and stomach.

People were watching.

The kids started crying.

I managed to crawl out the far side and stepped into someone's trolley.

They had left a child in the seat part and I toppled it over.

The child skidded across the floor and banged its head on a low shelf with raisins.

And I ran.

I ran down aisles of food and drink, past the cash desks, through the car park, through traffic lights, and down rows of houses past pubs.

I jumped on a bus and told the conductor town please.

The bus was packed with weekend shoppers.

I sat down beside a fat lady and knew I had to get pissed.

I went into the Flowing Tide on Abbey Street.

Pint and a short.

And a pint and a short.

Washing the burn of the whiskey away with beer.

My energy was coming back.

I wanted everything to just be okay.

If I could go back in time.

I've never felt so lonely.

I thought about ringing Phil and Declan, but I knew they were doing overtime, and there was no way I was ringing work.

No way.

Pint and a short.

Morning turned to afternoon.

I left to get a bite.

I was numb.

I crossed over by the Abbey down towards the quays.

An itinerant, a big man with short hair, was being held on the ground by two guards.

He was crying.

He shouted at a woman, "Don't leave me here, you'll break my heart."

She was going around the corner with a kid in a pram.

She stopped and shouted something back at him.

I didn't hear what it was but the man let his head fall on the pavement and his body was heaving with sobs.

He was a big man.

After seeing that, I needed to get to the south side.

It's nicer.

I was starving.

I love tuna salad, like in a sandwich or a roll. Subs and Salads, South Anne Street.

Straight out of there into Kehoes nearby.

It was pretty full.

I was the only one on my own.

A man at the bar was telling his friends about Monopoly. Everyone goes round the board fifty times or whatever.

And you've made ten grand and you've made two. But look at the board, he said.

The odd hotel or house, but the board's still the same. Nothing's changed and people have made a fortune. What's been bought or sold?

He said it made you think about ownership.

What does it mean to own something?

Something you take for granted.

What does it mean, yours or mine?

It was making me think, so I split.

People tried to sell me stuff on Grafton Street, down Suffolk Street, across Dame Street and into Temple Bar.

I went down to the Norseman and I got lucky.

Phil and Declan had just arrived.

My eye must've been a bit red, they asked me what happened.

I didn't want to talk about it so when they asked how Maria took the news I wriggled out of it.

We got a round.

I found out that Meaney hadn't said anything.

He came to work with his car fixed, and the office window had been repaired that morning.

There was a new terminal on my desk.

We talked about how much better off I was without the job.

The three of us would go into business together. Have a delivery service, driving all around the country with the windows down. And on the continent we'd sleep in the trucks.

They wouldn't let me buy a drink and I suppose that was decent.

I had about ten quid to my name.

I wondered what Maria would do for money.

She probably had some put away.

She was bound to.

There'd be a dinner on the table.

I stopped worrying.

We had toasted sandwiches and plenty of pints.

The evening began to turn and the pub was filling up.

Declan said his girlfriend was in the Stag's Head and we decided to go up.

As we left the Norseman I had a terrible feeling which I can only describe as homesickness.

I suddenly wanted to play with the kids or have a bath with Maria sitting on the toilet talking to me.

I put it down to being drunk.

Get a few more pints inside me and I'd be happy as a pig in shit.

It was ten. Early days. Go home later. Give things a chance to settle for God's sake.

The Stag's Head was black.

People sat in the street drinking.

Declan's girlfriend was downstairs with her Danish friend.

They were wrecked.

We got some pints and everyone was having a laugh, but I just listened and smoked Phil's cigarettes.

I was looking at the punters.

Young people.

Students.

And then I saw this girl.

She was beautiful.

She had long hair past her shoulders.

Straight shiny brown.

I liked the way she was casual.

White sweater, leggings, pair of boots.

She was smoking and talking to some idiot.

He had glasses and was dressed completely in black.

He was all animated talking about a play he was writing about the IRA.

She was just smoking and looking at him.

I thought to myself, If I could be with that girl she could cure my life.

I'd never have to worry about anything—what could go wrong?

At last orders I got a pint and a short.

The place was spinning.

I felt like I was in a big sleeping bag and I was looking at everything through a magnifying glass.

I wanted the lovely girl to look after me.

But I couldn't see her.

The Danish girl said she had tickets for us all to go and see Bjorn Again at midnight at the Olympia.

The barmen were kicking us out.

One of them shouted at me.

The others didn't notice.

I went upstairs to look for the girl, but she was gone.

I got sick in the street and waited for everyone.

I knew I couldn't go home in this state.

Two blokes asked me if I wanted hash.

I found I couldn't talk very well.

One of them gave me a dig and they started laughing.

I fell over and felt something wet.

It was where I'd been sick.

I think I lay there for a few minutes.

The next thing I remember is Phil picking me up and Declan saying, "He needs a drink."

I couldn't think or see straight.

Dame Street moved around my head.

I staggered along between the lads.

The Danish girl wiped my face.

I found it hard to keep my eyes open.

I got sick again and felt a little better. Phil told me I'd have to walk into the Olympia unsupported or none of us would get in.

I walked very slowly past the bouncers pretending to be listening to something Declan's girlfriend was saying.

For some reason I said, "Crane operator," and laughed but I can't remember what the joke was now.

The Danish girl handed over the tickets and we were in.

Our seats were upstairs.

The music hadn't started yet.

I fell into my seat and closed my eyes.

Then a cold drink in a paper cup was in my hand.

It was a concoction Declan claimed had power to wake the dead.

A rum and vodka with ice.

I took a gulp and a jolt shot through me.

I was sitting beside Miss Denmark.

Phil was kissing her.

He was licking her face.

One hand was up her skirt and the other one was on her tit.

A bouncer tapped Phil's shoulder and told him to cut it out.

He had to tell a lot of people.

Declan and Siobhan came back with another drink for me and said I looked a lot better.

Well I was awake.

Most of the people there were between thirty and forty.

Civil servanty types.

Nurses and guards.

Everybody was pissed.

People fell down the stairs or got sick in their seats.

There were a lot of really camp people too.

They spoke loudly and laughed at people they pointed out to each other.

A voice announced that the show involved a strobe light as a warning to people who who took fits.

A man in a yellow T-shirt shouted, "I'm an epileptic, I'm an epileptic." And everybody laughed.

I didn't think it was very funny.

Bjorn Again came out and sounded exactly like Abba. They looked like them and moved like them. It was uncanny.

It was good for about half an hour but the joke wore off and it got boring.

I wandered off to the bar.

I found I still couldn't walk very well—it was hard to keep my balance.

Everything looked like it was on telly.

There was a group of young people down at the front dancing around and having a really good time.

Would they think I was one of the stupid fuckers falling around in my Argyll sweater? Feeling my fat girlfriend's tits in front of everybody?

Didn't they see that I was different?

I wanted to go down on the stage, grab a microphone and scream at everyone that none of what was happening to me was my fault.

I could've done a lot with myself.

I'm an intelligent bloke.

But of course, I didn't.

I got a rum and vodka at the bar after pushing about for ten minutes with housewives and queers.

In the confusion I managed not to pay.

The bar was jammed.

People paying in to drink.

But they had money to burn.

Fat bastards.

And then I saw the girl from the Stag's Head. A man about thirty-five, thirty-six was talking very earnestly to her.

Every now and then she'd smile and shake her head. The man took a step backwards and held out his arms like he wanted her to search him or something.

I leaned against the wall and had a smoke.

I was watching her.

She was gorgeous.

Her skin was really clear, and when she smiled there were creases beside her eyes making her look a lot older.

I figured her for about nineteen or twenty.

Her eyes were wide set.

Not like she was a mutant or anything.

Just, I can't describe people.

You could see her eyes.

My heart was thumping.

I gulped my drink and moved closer to hear what they were saying.

And when I heard her speak I knew she was the girl for me.

She was experienced, worldly, she could look after me.

The man was talking about his missus.

She was screwing his neighbor.

So it was nothing personal.

He just wanted to get even.

In his own head.

I winced and the girl saw me and smiled.

She smiled at me.

He went on and on.

They could get a hotel room, have a meal.

I made a face. "Is this guy for real?"

She smiled at me again.

Because she was smiling the bloke thought he had a chance.

She could have a nice breakfast in bed.

A jacuzzi, and come-on, he wasn't that bad looking was he? She smiled at me again, then she walked over and held my hand.

She was holding my hand.

The bloke said something about the place being full of lesbians and went back to the bar.

She looked at me and said thanks.

Then she made to go back to the show, but I held her hand and tried speaking to her.

"What?" she was saying, "what?"

"Cure my life," I said.

"I want you to cure my life.

"I think you're beautiful."

I burst into tears and everyone was looking at me.

She dragged me out of the bar and down to the girls' toilets.

There were some women in there doing their hair and makeup or whatever.

I told them to fuck off before they could tell me I was in the wrong jacks.

We went into a cubicle and she asked me if I was alright.

I couldn't stop crying.

I felt too sorry for myself and I was enjoying it too much.

Poor me . . .

I grabbed her and she gave me a hug.

And inside my head a little voice said, "Hello . . . nice tits."

She was asking me what the matter was but I was beginning to feel more horny than upset.

"I'm okay," I said.

She said we should really get out of there.

Outside we met some of her friends.

Few guys, few girls.

The blokes looked like Bohemian film producers, the girls looked like a bunch of monkeys hooked on crack.

These people were very intense.

Even when they were trying to be funny.

But while she was talking to them she kept holding my hand.

I wasn't feeling horny then.

Just comfortable.

This was all very exciting.

We dumped the losers.

She wanted to know what the matter was but I just asked if we could go.

She didn't say anything.

She just led me down to where her coat was.

Her pals looked at me when she said she was off.

I gave them a moody scowl.

Couldn't they see there was a silent bond, a communication beyond words going on here?

Cunts.

We left the Olympia.

On the way out she squeezed my hand and smiled at me.

She was curing my life.

She hailed a taxi and I bundled in the back.

. . . Yes . . . she got in beside me.

. . . Okay.

She gave the guy an address.

I asked her where she lived.

She said Clontarf.

She lived with her parents but they were away.

"Is that where I'm going?" I asked her.

"Is that where you want to go?" she said.

I put my arm around her and she snuggled into me.

She was slender.

We sped through town.

People tried to flag our taxi.

I saw fights.

Men and women fighting.

Arguments outside chippers.

Drunks asleep in the street.

Down North Strand.

People walking home.

It was starting to rain.

And I was safe in the taxi with the woman I loved.

Through Fairview.

Along the coast.

The tide was out.

Rubbish all along the shore.

Now it was lashing.

I was nice and warm.

We turned left up by Clontarf Castle.

And stopped outside a huge house.

"That's six pounds even."

The girl paid.

She helped me out of the car.

The front door was a huge slab of oak.

A dark house, smelled musty.

Smelled like the sea.

We were in the sitting room.

Two plush green suites.

Carpets thick as your finger.

Patio doors led to a wide garden. Everything was quiet.

She asked me if I wanted a drink.

A big rum and vodka, with lots of ice.

She had a beer.

We sat there smoking in the lamplight.

"What am I doing here?" I asked her.

"What do you want to do?" she said.

She took my hand and led me upstairs.

A square open landing.

Her door, a room at the back.

A big bed, a table full of books.

Wooden varnished floor.

Her own bathroom en suite.

I asked if I could take a shower.

She said of course.

I locked the door and took a big shit.

I turned on the shower and undressed.

My feet on the tiles.

I saw myself in the mirror.

I looked like I was dead.

Like I'd been beaten to death.

I scrubbed myself from top to bottom.

I was pissed out of my head.

I felt okay.

I dried myself with a nice towel.

My clothes were manky.

I put on her robe and went into the bedroom.

She was in bed.

I was trembling all over.

"You getting in?" she asked me.

I shut the bathroom door and took off the robe.

She pulled back the quilt and I climbed in.

The bed was warm.

She lay on top of me and started kissing my neck.

It was too late now.

My willy went boing.

She laughed and grabbed it.

"What's your name?" I asked her.

"Myfanwy," she said. "It's Welsh."

PART TWO

The first thing I remember about waking up is that horrible feeling like you're falling off a cliff.

Everything came flooding back like a kick in the bollocks.

I was lying in a room that shouted money, in bed with a rich girl called Myfanwy.

I checked her bedside clock.

Quarter to ten.

Twelve hours ago I was thinking about going home.

What had happened? The sun was blazing through the window.

Myfanwy was asleep with her back to me.

I could barely remember what she looked like.

I thought about what a slut she was taking a complete stranger to her bed.

The more I thought about it the more disgusted I was.

I'm a married man.

Even if she had no respect for me, at least she should have thought about my wife.

I dozed, and when I looked at the clock again it was eleven.

My head was exploding.

I needed some painkillers or a drink, or both.

My clothes were on the bathroom floor.

I put on her robe and took my stuff downstairs to the washing machine.

I threw everything in except my shoes.

I'm not even going to try describing what kind of shape I was in.

Every movement was an effort.

I found some paracetamol and opened a beer.

Our glasses were where we had left them in the sitting room.

I sat there in someone else's house drinking their beer.

There were photographs on the walls.

Weddings, graduations, black and whites.

I felt like an intruder.

I looked at their videos and their CDs.

I tried playing their piano.

I lay under their coffee table.

They never could have guessed that all the stuff they took for granted would ever receive this much attention.

I was still drunk.

Maria would think I stayed in Phil and Declan's.

I could go home and make it up to her.

I didn't quite know how, but I would.

I was going to sacrifice all my free time and show her I was sorry.

But what was I sorry for? I couldn't go back to my job.

I just couldn't.

She was the one who hit me in Crazy Prices.

I don't think I deserved that.

I didn't know what to do.

I went upstairs.

Myfanwy was still asleep.

I wanted to get out.

I wished I hadn't put my clothes in the machine.

I could've split.

There was a pair of pink tracksuit bottoms on the back of a chair.

I put them on and got a pair of tiny socks out of a drawer.

I found a T-shirt and got my shoes.

The sun was baking down.

I left the door on the latch, and strolled up the road.

I went around by the cricket club and down Belgrove Road as far as Vernon Avenue.

Then I turned right.

Down to the seafront.

Clontarf is beautiful.

Old houses and trees, the breeze comes over the sea, and there's a ghost on every corner.

People were coming and going to mass.

I went down the coast and into the Dollymount house.

It was huge. A boozerama.

I got a pint and a short and sat at a window looking at the bay curving round to Howth.

You could see everything clearly.

It was peaceful.

I wished I was on top of Howth Head, looking at Dublin.

I wished it was a couple of years ago and I was making plans instead of just drifting with whatever went on.

I had another pint and it made a huge difference.

I felt much better.

I had about four quid to my name.

I knew I wanted to get pissed before holy hour so I mooched back along the coast to Myfanwy's road.

I heard a radio in the kitchen when I pushed the big front door open.

"Is that you?" she shouted.

"Yeah," I said, because I'm witty like that.

She bounded to the kitchen door and looked out at me.

She started laughing and told me my clothes would be ready soon.

She asked me if I was hungry.

I said a sandwich would be fine.

We sat in the kitchen for a while.

She gave me a can of beer and asked me where I'd gone.

When I told her she said I drink too much. She wanted to know who was playing the piano at the crack of dawn.

I said it wasn't me, and she said no, it was nice.

She started asking me about myself.

She didn't even know my name.

I said it was Michael.

She wanted to know where I lived and worked.

I couldn't answer her.

I knew she had her suspicions, but I'm a coward and I asked her questions instead.

She'd been a student at Trinity.

She had a degree in Italian and something else.

She was going to do a business diploma.

I asked her if she had a hangover.

She said she hadn't been drinking.

For some reason I found that perverse.

I told her I wanted to go into town.

She gave my clothes a shot in the drier.

I had another beer and ate my sandwich.

I didn't feel like talking much.

She sat on my lap and started kissing me but I didn't feel much like that either.

She said I'd changed my tune since last night, and did I not think she was beautiful anymore?

Of course, talking about last night she might as well have been talking about the Boer War as far as I held myself responsible.

I told her I was tired and maybe later.

But her parents were coming home later she said.

I know this seems shitty, but if I was going to get pissed I had to stay on her good side and time was ticking away.

I spent half an hour banging her on the sitting room floor.

Then she ironed my pants and I was going mad because it was half one.

CONOR MCPHERSON

We'd never make it in time.

She laughed and said we'd take her car.

She had a fucking car.

She turned on the alarm and took her mini out of the garage.

Zoom.

She was a pretty good driver.

We were sitting in Davy Byrne's (her choice) at ten to two.

We both had pints.

Then I had a pint and a short.

Then I had another pint and Myfanwy had a glass. She paid. She knew.

We were finally kicked out at half two.

That felt much better.

And only another hour and a half till the next one.

Myfanwy asked if I was okay.

"Oh yeah, fine."

She asked what I wanted to do now.

I didn't mind.

We walked around for a while.

Around Merrion Square and St. Stephen's Green.

She asked me questions.

At the start when I wouldn't answer she thought it was sort of fun, but I could see it was beginning to annoy her now.

She was bored with the mystery man.

I felt rotten about it.

We sat down in a place on South Anne Street for something to eat.

I told her everything that had happened over the last two days.

She was excited.

She liked me.

I impressed her.

She didn't mind that I was married or anything.

I told her about my daughters.

But then I had to stop.

It was none of her fucking business.

She wanted to know if there was anything she could do.

I said, "No . . . just keep paying."

She laughed and put her arms around me. After she had held on to me for a minute she looked at me, but although she was smiling she was a bit tearful for some reason.

I suppose it was a bit sad.

It was still very warm so we took our coffee outside.

We sat at a table like garden furniture and she said she thought I should ring my wife.

But I was too embarrassed and guilty.

She wanted to know if she could see me again. I didn't know.

Anyway she said, we had the rest of the day.

There was a party in Rathmines that night and would I go.

Of course, I said I would.

Anything to avoid thinking about going home just yet.

Then a group of Myfanwy's friends came along.

Everybody wanted to hug Myfanwy.

I think they reckoned I was just someone sitting at her table.

They seemed a bit surprised when she introduced me.

There was Rupert, a huge bloke who looked like an officer in the SS.

Feargal, a squatty little guy with glasses that had a cord going 'round the back of his neck.

Sorcha, who looked like a model.

Jane, who had a complexion like dark cream.

And Sinead, who spoke Irish as much as she could.

They all got coffee.

My buzz was wearing off but Myfanwy seemed to want to stay there.

Rupert was at acting school.

His class were doing a modern version of King Oedipus and everybody had to go.

He had learned so much about himself since the start of rehearsals.

There's nothing in modern drama that isn't in Greek tragedy and comedy.

I asked him what the theatre had to do with real life.

I thought he'd have an answer seeing as he was at a school and everything.

But he went on for about ten minutes and it was very boring.

I can't remember what he said.

Then he started to explain why comedy is funny breaking it down into some Russian cunt's three "levels" of humor.

No one laughed.

He kept touching Myfanwy's hand.

I wanted for me and her to go and get sloshed.

Sorcha was a model.

She had done an ad for shampoo where no one saw her face, just the back of her head.

Then a fight broke out when Feargal said he thought Christy Turlington looked like a baboon.

They talked about Rwanda.

Friends of theirs abroad.

A girl they knew was pregnant.

A lecturer at Trinity who wore pink cords.

They spoke about how the country would never forgive Dick Spring for going into government with Albert.

And I wanted a pint.

I knew I was as intelligent as these fuckers.

But I just didn't seem to have any opinions.

I was embarrassed sitting there.

I eventually got the nerve to ask Myfanwy to come for a drink.

To my dismay, everyone thought this was a great idea.

We went to the International Bar.

Going down Grafton Street and Wicklow Street Myfanwy held my hand.

I was shitting someone I knew would see me.

I wasn't enjoying myself.

I sat back in the pub and let Myfanwy do the buying.

She did the necessary.

She was curing my life.

Her friends drank a pint an hour.

Myfanwy and I drank steadily.

Pace is the secret.

I was feeling a little better.

I was talking to Jane, the girl with the complexion like dark cream.

I told her a joke about niggers and she lost the head.

I didn't talk to her again.

And then Feargal and her left to collect Feargal's kid from his ex-girlfriend.

I asked Sorcha if being a model meant people treated her like a bimbo, or a good-looking object.

She said no and I didn't pursue it.

I was bored.

Myfanwy got me a rum and vodka.

Rupert told us about a film script he was writing with a friend of his from college.

It was about a girl who wants to be an artist but lacks the confidence.

He wanted to set it in Paris and have it done in French.

It would be more beautiful.

I asked if he spoke French.

He said not really but it was going to be subtitled.

I didn't understand, but he'd had three pints so I let it go.

He told us he found women more interesting than men.

He wanted to be a woman.

He wasn't gay or anything.

He just thought women have better insights and if they ran things the world wouldn't be as fucked-up.

I told him I thought he was a prick.

But Myfanwy laughed and the others thought it was a joke.

It turned out to be Rupert's party we were going to.

They left for his house to get things ready.

It was dusk and the pub was nearly empty.

Myfanwy put her head on my shoulder and told me she didn't know what to say.

I told her that was alright, because I wasn't interested anyway.

She laughed and held me.

Then we got up and went out to her mini.

We stopped on George Street and Myfanwy gave me a fiver to get fags.

I bought two packs.

Camel lights and Gauloises.

I was being a classy guy I explained to Myfanwy.

"Mmm . . ." she said, "mind if we take a detour?"

We drove to Ranelagh and stopped outside a house Myfanwy said was her brother's.

She was going to dress me properly.

Her brother was in Pakistan writing a history textbook.

We went up to his bedroom.

She opened the huge wardrobe and started throwing things onto the bed.

Hundreds of pounds' worth of shirts.

A jacket that cost five hundred pounds.

A tie that cost seventy pounds.

And that's what I'm wearing now.

I don't think it does much for me but it felt classy at the time.

While I was standing there half undressed Myfanwy started feeling me up.

I knew what I had to do and I did it.

We were back in the car at ten.

I took a bottle of vodka from her brother's drink cabinet.

We could hear the music coming from Rupert's house from down the road where we were parked.

He had the house to himself and there were people in every window.

We walked in past people drinking in the garden.

A couple were snogging in the hall.

We went into the kitchen.

Myfanwy was talking to some friends of hers in the doorway.

I sat at the kitchen table and poured some vodka into a mug.

A bunch of lads from the country asked for a sup.

I passed them the bottle and they slugged out of it.

Some blokes over at the back door kept going out for a joint.

I don't think they were afraid of being caught, they just didn't want to share it.

Another bloke was standing at the cooker making himself some soup.

A girl stood behind him with her hands in his front pockets.

Two girls and a bloke stood in front of me at the table talking about films I'd never heard of.

I went to have a look around.

The music was all techno.

There were people in the living room going mad to it.

MTV was on with the sound down.

Myfanwy was dancing.

She looked fabulous.

She had a sleeveless check shirt and a pair of shorts.

Rupert was dancing like he'd just been let out of a mental home.

A young couple sat on the floor in a corner.

They were having a shit time.

The girl made half-arsed attempts to get her boyfriend up to dance but you could see neither of them really wanted to.

I sat down with them and we shared the bottle.

The girl took a smoke.

I wanted to know what was wrong with them.

I wanted them to relax and cheer up. It sort of became important to me.

They kept saying they were alright but I knew they were fucked.

What was it about them?

I don't know.

"I hope it'll be okay," I said.

"That's all I'm going to say to you."

I went to pour them more drink but the bottle was gone.

We looked around.

Someone had taken it.

Then the girl saw it.

The muckers from the country had it.

They were sitting on the couch talking to a very beautiful girl.

If they had asked I would've given them some.

The girl said she was going to ask them to give it back.

"No," I said. "Don't ask."

I stood up and bent over the couple. I shook the guy's hand and kissed the girl on her forehead.

I was a bit upset.

I went over to the couch.

The muckers looked at me.

One of them had the bottle between his legs trying to hide it.

I grabbed it away from him and swung it at his face.

The bottom of it hit his nose right on the bridge.

That really fucked-up his face.

The bottle hadn't smashed so I heaved it against the side of another bloke's head.

It broke with a pop and glass went everywhere.

Someone screamed.

I went to find Myfanwy.

We were going.

She wasn't in the kitchen or out the back.

She wasn't on the stairs or in the toilet.

There was no one in the first bedroom. A pair of eejits were playing guitars in the next one.

The lights were off in the third.

Bad news.

I found the switch.

Myfanwy was on the bed.

Her shirt was open and her shorts were around her feet.

Rupert's head was between her legs.

He was kneeling on the floor pulling himself off.

The first thought that went through my head was, He's licking my spunk.

Myfanwy saw me and started kicking him away.

But he kept a hold of her.

I started laughing.

He lifted his head up and said, "Squeeze your tits, I'm coming."

He saw me and came.

Myfanwy rolled over and put her head in her hands.

Rupert pulled the quilt off the bed and covered himself.

"Good-bye," I said.

The lights were all on downstairs and the music had stopped.

People brought towels in and out of the living room.

I saw Myfanwy's jacket on a chair beside the hall phone.

I took her wallet and left.

The night was warm.

Myfanwy had twenty quid.

I hailed a taxi and said, "Raheny please."

"You were walking the wrong way mate," he said.

We drove through town, through Fairview, up the Howth Road, across Sibyl Hill and into Raheny Village.

"This is fine," I said.

I was hungry so I went over to the chipper.

It was about twelve o clock and the chipper was packed.

There were two men in front of me who were about forty.

They were wrecked.

One of them had a little girl with him who was about two.

She was sleepy and crying.

He was asking her if she wanted chips.

Then he told his friend he was dead.

His missus would kill him.

I didn't feel hungry after that.

I made my way back to the estate.

One or two people were walking back from the pub.

All the houses the same.

Each one with a mortgage.

Each one with a love story.

I opened the front door quietly and crept upstairs.

Everything was like a tomb.

I went into my daughters.

I sat on the floor and listened to them breathing.

Their fair hair and white cotton pajamas.

Their little hands.

I couldn't bear it.

End of Play

AFTERWORD

RUM AND VODKA
NOVEMBER 1992

Rum and Vodka premiered in November 1992 at University
College Dublin where I was completing an M.A. in philosophy.
I wrote the play when I was twenty. It was the first monologue
I wrote. Up until then I'd been doing normal ensemble plays
with lots of characters talking to each other endlessly. These
plays were written with perhaps a sense of wanting to be a
playwright rather than wanting to be a good writer. But *Rum
and Vodka* is the play with which I think I found my voice.

I directed a student friend, Stephen Walshe, in the first
production. He was a commerce student with a great inter-
est in theatre. It never occurred to me that a full-length
monologue might be difficult for an actor to learn. I just
thought it would be like telling a long joke. You don't have
to be word perfect as long as people are getting the gist. Of
course this was bullshit. If you forget your lines, it's a night-
mare. Someone who was being so lucid a minute ago is suddenly stammering like a terrified donkey.

Some time later Brian Cox dried in a production of my
monologue, *St. Nicholas*, in London. Years of experience gave

him the confidence to merely turn to the crowd and say, "I'm terribly sorry, ladies and gentlemen, I wonder would you mind very much if I started again?" As he was only about six minutes in, nobody seemed to care, in fact many people said they found it very exciting to have this happen. However, one woman reviewing the play for BBC radio did complain about this mishap, as though Brian was an athlete who was expected to perform like an automaton. Live theatre always has the possibility of turning into a mess, and that's part of it. That's part of the fun.

But back to *Rum and Vodka*. Stephen Walshe had a photographic memory. He told me he could literally see the page in front of him as he spoke to the audience. He was "reading" it.

Lots of people came to see it and we had a good time. So when the opportunity arose to do the play again for a week at Trinity College in the center of Dublin, we jumped at the chance. But there was a slight problem. The week we were given was right before the summer exams, so we were playing to literally nobody. One night only one young woman showed up, and she didn't seem to have great English. My friend, Colin O'Connor, and I went up to the dressing room to tell Stephen we were pulling the show. But Stephen said he wanted to do it. Colin and I were having the same thought: giving a long monologue to one foreign person was a bit weird and embarrassing. But Stephen wanted to do it. Finally we persuaded him that it was a much better idea to go and get drunk instead. I went to tell the foreign girl that the show was off. She too seemed quite disappointed, and she wandered off on her own. I still feel a bit stupid that I never invited her to come with us. But that might have been even weirder, sitting there in the pub explaining the play to her.

About a year later, some ex-students offered us a week to do *Rum and Vodka* in the basement of a café on Dublin's Quays. Again Stephen was mad eager to do it. This was a smelly little place and the "lighting cues" consisted of switching the light on and off just like you would at home. Considering the bad language in the play I never wanted anyone watching

the play who was too young. But one night, to my horror,
I saw a ten-year-old kid sitting in the audience. I went and
complained to the people at the door, but their argument
was that they'd managed to charge him a full price ticket.

The next production of the play was at The City Arts
Centre, directed by Colin O'Connor. Everything was going
quite well until the day of the artistic director's wedding,
when some arsehole nicked the costume to wear to the do.
Again it was a case of pulling the show for that evening.
Oh well. Pub? Any excuse.

THE GOOD THIEF
APRIL 1994

The Good Thief was first performed by an actor friend, Kevin
Hely, under the title *The Light of Jesus*. We did it in a real theatre in Dublin, which cost us a fortune because nobody
came. We did get some great reviews but no one knew who
we were and the title was so off-putting. We hired slide projectors and displayed slides all the way through the show.
These changed like any technical cue—when Kevin said a
certain line we'd click one or other of the projectors, dis-
playing something relevant to the narrative. Some pictures
were fairly literal and others were ironic. And it was a pretty
cool effect. The only drawback was that if Kevin made a
mistake or lost his place in the story, the slides would be out
of synch. They were loaded into the projectors in such a
way that we'd never really have time to change the order they
came in. At this time, Kevin, a Fly by Night member since
the beginning, was holding down a job teaching computer
science. He was also shooting a no-budget feature film in
which he was playing the lead. In other words, he was
knackered. We decided to open the show without any previews so we could be reviewed as soon as possible, gambling
that we'd get critically acclaimed and sell out instantly. Ha ha.

What this practically meant was that we never gave

Kevin a chance to publicly perform a full-length monologue before opening night.

He fainted on stage.

Everything was going fine until about half an hour in. I suddenly sensed that Kevin was about to forget his lines. It's weird with actors, you just know that they're going to "dry" before it happens. You just think to yourself, "You're gone. I can see it. You know about the next two lines, and then it's the abyss." Kevin simply stopped talking and wandered over to the side of the stage where he sank to the floor and leaned against a pillar. Now had either of us been more experienced, I would have shouted his next line at him. But we felt, I suppose, that a loud prompt would ruin "the illusion" we pretentiously thought we were creating. So I sat there beside one of the slide projectionists, Jason Byrne, and just gripped his arm. Years later he said he could still feel me nearly breaking his bones with terror. It seemed like minutes before Kevin started talking again—it was in fact a few seconds. The weird thing was, after the show people said they didn't remember this happening, or they just thought it was part of the play.

We performed to thin houses for two weeks and finished up losing whatever money we'd put in. And that should have been that. But there was an amount of enthusiasm from people asking us to give it another go somewhere else. And believe it or not, a theatre critic (!) set up a proper showcase for us at the Project Arts Centre. His name was Mic Moroney. He invited lots of journalist pals and people who worked in the proper theatre. Among them was a cousin of mine, Garrett Keogh, a professional actor who was well known in Ireland at the time because he was playing a villain in a soap opera called *Fair City*. He suggested to me that he perform the play, with me directing, and that we do it in the Dublin Theatre Festival.

I agreed and Garrett found a coproducer: self-styled Dublin film editor, Se Merry Doyle. Se and Garrett had been friends for many years. Se loved the play and it was decided that they'd produce it in a new student union build-

ing in Temple Bar. As a venue it was designed for kids to drink
and dance, i.e., it was a concrete bunker. Se and Garrett
decided This Is Going To Be An Event. Opening a theatre
where there hadn't been one before. This was really exciting.
I was twenty-three and all this mad stuff was happening. New
slide photography was commissioned. Entire banks of seats
were built. A set designer was hired. The Abbey Theatre's
lighting man was called in. I'd never done anything on this
scale. My job was to help Garrett prepare for his role. This
would be easy. Working with good actors is never very hard.

One day, walking down to the theatre, Garrett said,
"You know no one is going to come and see a play called
The Light of Jesus, don't you?" "Fuck them," I replied, all
flushed and idealistic. All theatrical. We walked a little further in silence, down past Bewleys on Westmoreland Street.
Then Garrett turned to me with a strange mixture of concern and amusement, "Do you know you're on ten percent
of the box office takings?" I had a little think, which led to
a little mumble, "Well . . . I . . . had thought before about
calling it . . . *The . . . Good Thief.*"

"Perfect," said Garrett.

By the time we opened Garrett and Se had managed to
create a bit of buzz. There was a wine reception. Frank
McGuinness formally opened the "theatre." In the program
was a letter of congratulations from the Minister of Arts.
Boozy journalists stared dourly at the proceedings. I stood
joking with relatives and friends. Very nervous. When the
play started, I stayed behind the audience, listening. And as
soon as I knew there weren't going to be any disasters I went
and stood at the bar with the chap who ran the building.

Some reviews were spectacular. And some were fairly
shitty. The run never really took off. Some nights were
three-quarters full, some were almost empty. Money was
lost. Tensions began to generate. Garrett and Se finally fell
out over a missing lens cap for a pair of binoculars one had
borrowed from the other. Many nights during the run I
slipped around to the Festival club for a late drink. One

night I made a point of thanking a critic profusely for giving us a scathing review. He wasn't sure if I was making a mistake but couldn't bring himself to correct me. He was in agony. Meanwhile, our slide projectionist, Jason Byrne, got into a row with another unfavorable critic. We were toughening up. And when the run farted to an undistinguished close, I again thought, Well, that's the end of that.

But a few weeks later, Garrett had come up with a surefire money-maker, a national tour. The Arts Council in Ireland gives rural venues money to pay for touring productions to come and visit. Once the venue decides they'd like you to perform, they give you a guaranteed payment, even if no audience turns up. So we went back into rehearsals and slimmed the whole thing down. No more slide projection nonsense. All we needed was a chair, and the tour began.

I went to see it in a couple of places and my most memorable time was at the Playhouse in Derry.

Garrett always had a whiskey bottle on stage while he performed and drank from it regularly. It contained apple juice. It looked like whiskey and it was easy to drink. But when we arrived in Derry our stage manager, Philip, couldn't find any apple juice in the shops. Garrett said he had to drink something. The show was starting in like ten minutes. We thought about what might work. Cold tea? No, disgusting. Red lemonade? No, too much fizz. What then? Garrett sighed and reached into his pocket. He handed me a ten. "Get me a bottle of whiskey," he said. And I did.

When I handed it to him he went to open it. "No," I said, "Open it on stage in front of the audience. Let them hear the seal break. Let them know it's real." And that's what happened. He opened it on stage and the mad bastard drank about half the bottle. Was he pissed? Well, let's just say there were a right few pauses towards the end of the show. But he did it and it was fine. Afterwards, me and Garrett and Philip polished the bottle off in the dressing room and then we went to the pub. As usual I got stuck talking to some headcheese. Garrett was talking to an ex-UVF prisoner and getting on great. At closing time we went into a pizza take-away place where Half-Bottle-Of-Whiskey-Boy bought about ten pizzas for these middle-aged women he was suddenly best friends with. He was flying. Outside I was trying to persuade him not to get into a taxi with them. He had a show to do in Monaghan the next evening. But he knew best. And off he went.

Dr. Jekyll met Mr. Hyde in the morning. Garrett was a pale, shivering imitation of the man he used to be. It turned out that he'd gone back to a house in Derry's Republican stronghold, the Bogside. He'd been sitting there drinking with these women, thinking he was getting on fairly well, when there was a bang at the door. And in came four big lads in leather jackets. It was three o'clock in the morning and Garrett was there with their girlfriends. Considering both the hour and where they were, saying these men probably knew how to handle themselves had to be something of an understatement. So what did Garrett do? Did he behave himself? Did he ingratiate himself? Explain himself?

The way he told me, his thought process was this: "This could be a bad situation. Something must be done to make sure it isn't. The best thing to do is take control. I'll be pre-emptive and confuse them." So without a word being said, he leapt up and threw a few kung fu moves at them. Now, like a lot of people who pull stunts like this, Garrett didn't know kung fu. And it was probably lucky for him that he didn't. Because the lads never moved. They just stood there for a moment and then they started laughing at him and gave him a beer. This goes to show something. I don't know what though. It's often hard to learn from a true original.

So that morning we set out to drive to Monaghan. Bruce Lee decided he should lie in the back of the car and sleep for the journey. But he was still a bit off his face, chatting away and telling us jokes and stories and spoofs. And every time Boyzone came on the radio singing "Love Me for a Reason," Garrett goes, "There's your song, Conor." In Monaghan we got Garrett some food. He ate some steak and chips and then finally went for a snooze in the car.

It turned out that I was going to be operating the lights for the show, which was a fairly simple task. They came up at the beginning and went down at the end. Poor Garrett struggled gamely on. I'm being unfair. He was great. Until the last line. All along, during the run in Dublin, during the tour, his performance had been downbeat, subtle, he wasn't hitting everybody over the head with what he was saying, nor was he patronizingly leading them by the hand. But in Monaghan, in his weakened state and with diminished judgment, he decided to give the last line a little bit of quivering emotion. Just as he said, "I was trying to get out of the rain," he let his voice break. The tiniest sob, but enough. Enough to make me think, "What the fuck are you playing at?" And instead of bringing the lights down on his last line I left them at full power, leaving Garrett standing there with no more lines. Just standing there waiting for the blackout. Until I began the slowest fade, thinking, "Act now, you fucker . . ." Cruel, no?

THIS LIME TREE BOWER
SEPTEMBER 1995

Casting *Lime Tree Bower* was a new experience for me. Many of my friends from the Fly by Night Theatre Company were unavailable either because they had traveled abroad or they were being formally trained as actors at Trinity College. Trinity didn't allow their students to act in productions outside the course. So for the first time I had to actually get in touch with agents and say, "Send me actors to audition." And they did. Auditioning is something you need a bit of a technique for. You want to seem friendly, but not get anyone's hopes up too much. I usually decide in the first few minutes if someone can (a) Act and (b) Play the part. You know in the first few seconds when someone's wrong. But out of courtesy you give them the full twenty minutes or whatever.

I saw a few good people but the final decisions were relatively easy. I had already offered the part of the lecturer, Ray, to a Dublin actor, Conor Mullen. I'd seen him in a play at the Peacock and immediately knew he'd be brilliant. I accosted him in the pub across the road and met him a few days later when he'd read the script. One of the best decisions I've made. (If you ever get connected to the Irish telephone automated information system, it's Conor's voice you'll hear. Listen to the authority.)

The parts of Joe and Frank went to Ian Cregg and Niall Shanahan, respectively, two actors I found through audition. It's always incredible how the people who are right for the part just seem to appear ready made. You think, What the hell am I going to do for the next few weeks? They don't need me to tell them anything much. But it's about confidence. You spend time telling them they can do it. They should do it. This is the only thing they should ever do. And the fools buy it.

Because they all deliver monologues, I was working with them separately. They didn't see each other from the first read through until the final week of rehearsal. They'd ask me, "How are the others getting on?" And I'd say, "Okay. Not as good as you." When they finally met to rehearse the whole thing together they nearly jumped on each other with relief that they were all in the same boat. They were a great cast and a good bunch to have fun with.

We were playing in the Fringe Festival and the show was an immediate smash. We sold out every night. The cast was on profit share, and almost unbelievably for a fringe show, they got paid at the end. It wasn't much, considering they'd rehearsed for free too, but I was delighted there was no bad taste in anyone's mouth. In fact things got better.

At this time I was pretty much unemployed. I was writing but it wasn't paying. But a literary agent from London, Nick Marston, came to see *Lime Tree* and took me on, saying he felt theatres in London would be dying to stage it. This was cool, walking around saying things like, "Yeah, that's a pain in the ass. Actually, I was just saying to my agent in London, the other day . . ."

Within a fortnight offers to meet theatre bosses in London were coming through. I flew over. And there I was riding around on the tube between the Royal Court in Sloane Square and the Bush in Shepherd's Bush. And, in between, meeting my publisher. *Meeting my publisher!*

I suppose the start of good things is the best time. I remember that day very clearly. I knew I had come to some corner. I knew I go could back, but I didn't want to.

I decided to do the play at the Bush because they had no quibbles with me bringing the Dublin cast over. We came to London the following summer straight into blistering heat and pollution. Me and Niall Shanahan had terrible hayfever. We were all staying in different places for the first while. Ian was sleeping on someone's landing. Niall had a room in a house but there was no door in the frame.

The Bush theatre is a hundred-seater above a pub. After rehearsals we sat in the pub and went for Indian take-aways. And earlier in the year the Bush had asked me to become their writer-in-residence, which meant they paid me some money. I was also getting paid because my screenplay, *I Went Down*, was going into production. This felt nuts.

I remember me and Conor Mullen staying in digs near Stamford Brook. It was a house owned by a semi-retired actress, Sheila Burnette. She was very kind to us. There were strict rules, but once you obeyed them there were no problems. A very tranquil memory I have is waking up in blazing sunshine. My room faced the back garden. We had been out on the batter the night before. I could hear voices chatting away merrily outside. Down in the garden, stretched out on deck chairs, were Conor and Sheila sipping mid-morning gin and tonics, watching the planes landing and taking off from Heathrow. These two people just commenting on the planes in the sunshine. One of those moments when you think, that's the pace we should strive for.

Towards the end of rehearsals the lads were finally given

a house they could share. It was a nice place, small, terraced, with a conservatory at the back. There were two proper bedrooms and a half-converted attic with a ladder going up into it. Niall Shanahan always considered himself the unluckiest member of the cast. There was no reason why he should have been. He just seemed to project a kind of resignation. When the three boys came to draw lots for the rooms, he didn't even bother. He knew he'd get the attic. And he did.

Conor Mullen got the big bedroom. He was the opposite of Niall. He also had the most comfortable chair on stage. He didn't fight for it or anything. Conor just *seemed* right in that chair. It's hard to describe. They were all lovely blokes. They just had different levels of confidence. It was a fascinating dynamic. It was funny. Niall just felt like he deserved the worst room, the worst chair, the hottest costume.

But as soon as they started acting, they were completely their characters. Especially in London. Niall was unsettlingly confident as Frank. And Conor gave us intriguing glimpses of the insecurity behind Ray's brash, bullying exterior.

The first preview came along. I was certain it was going to be a disaster. I couldn't believe we'd made it that far and I still can't believe that Ian Cregg got up and started the play in front of a strange audience. I was like, What's wrong with these people? How the hell are we getting away with this? But we were and we did.

My Dad and my two sisters had traveled over from Dublin to be with me for the opening. When I met up with them before the first show, they had decided to take a taxi from their hotel to Shepherd's Bush right in the middle of rush hour. The trip had cost them something like fifty pounds. I was furious. I felt responsible. They didn't know London. I was the reason they were here. They were by no means wealthy and here they were getting ripped off, paying ten times what they'd have had to on the tube. And horribly, they didn't care as long as they could be with me for this important night. Somehow I knew things had changed. The stakes were all higher now. If things went well, the rewards

and opportunities would be great. If not, you were staring down a well of disappointment you could visit and draw from as much as you liked. And no one would bother you.

But the reviews were all great. Part of the satisfaction I drew from this, besides making some money and generally having a success, was the attention the actors were getting from high-powered agencies like ICM and PFD. Film and TV producers were coming to check them out with offers of auditions and screen tests for various projects. No longer were they sitting in the house or wandering around London before the show. They were reading scripts and going to meetings. Brilliant.

ST. NICHOLAS

FEBRUARY 1997

St. Nicholas was the play I wrote for the Bush as their writer-in-residence. It was a one-man play for a man in his fifties. I was to direct. I had long chats with the new artistic director, Mike Bradwell, about who should play it. It was difficult to know. We knew it needed someone with a strong presence who could give us bleak devastation and make it funny. I suggested that I'd had Brian Cox in mind when I wrote it. I'd even cut his picture out of a magazine and stuck it on the folder I was using for the play. As far as I was concerned this was wishful thinking. He was so busy doing films, and how could you persuade an Olivier award-winning actor to come to a pub and work for two hundred quid a week? Mike mulled it over and said, "I don't know. Let's send it to him. Brian's just about mad enough to do it."

So off the script went. To Hollywood. A few days later the phone rang: "Conor? This is Brian Cox. I want to give you my dates to see if we can work something out." I couldn't accept that this was happening so smoothly. I went out for a long walk. I walked for hours down on the beach in Dollymount. I got in after dark. A grinning idiot.

300

Given Brian's busy schedule we broke the rehearsal period up. One week on, two weeks off, another week, another break, and two weeks before opening. Consequently we rehearsed in a number of different places.

The first was Riverside Studios in Hammersmith. I didn't know Brian. I was nervous. He was very enthusiastic and put me at ease in rehearsal. We drank a lot of tea. This first week was quite lonely. I was in a town I didn't know very well and there wasn't a full cast to associate with. We had to rely on each other.

The weather was freezing, it was the first week in January and night fell at five o'clock. I'd sort of make my way halfheartedly back to my digs knowing full well I wouldn't be able to sit there for long. It felt like every night was Sunday night and I hadn't done my homework. So, I'd mooch down to Shepherd's Bush and annoy the Bush staff into coming out for a drink. I had a right couple of hangovers that week. And I reckon that helped me stop worrying about the fact that my play was about a theatre critic who falls in love with an actress and ends up working for vampires. I was too tired to worry.

The next place we rehearsed was a church hall in White City. We were very cold. There was a large fan heater but it made so much noise we couldn't work with it on. It heated the air rather than the room. You could leave it on for two hours and as soon as you turned it off, you might as well have been outside. (No, it was warmer outside.)

By this time there were more of us in the room, our assistant director Helen and our stage manager Zoe. Things were a bit more chatty. Brian told us stories about working in famous classical productions and Hollywood movies. And we just sort of drank our tea.

Brian was working with an accent coach from Dublin. For a week or two he sounded like he'd lived in a caravan in every county in Ireland, especially when he got tired. But he worked his bollocks off and began to sound quite good as the production neared. He reminded me of an uncle I had in Dublin.

We spoke about the play. We liked the character. He was honest. We felt sorry for him. We were afraid the critics would attack us for portraying one of their number in such a degrading fashion. I was also afraid they'd knock me for not writing an ensemble play which many of them suggested I do after my first Bush production, *This Lime Tree Bower*. We veered from strutting arrogance to stumbling cowardice and back again.

We started doing interviews.

Brian came to Dublin. We walked around the places where I imagined the play happened. We did some shopping. Brian tried his accent out.

The next place we rehearsed was Latvia House. This was a cultural center for Latvian expatriates near Hyde Park. I felt at home there. It might have been something to do with my Catholic upbringing. Latvia House was full of images: depictions of battles, portraits of dignitaries, emblems with birds on them. We were in a large first-storey room with a wooden floor and high windows, which opened onto a balcony where we could smoke.

There was a place nearby where we could get sandwiches and so on. Brian and I sat there one lunchtime and became intrigued with the waitress's accent. She was very beautiful, very dark, she sounded Eastern European. I told Brian she reminded me of what the vampires might be like in the play. Brian said, "She's Russian." He had done a lot of work in Russia and was a bit of a Russophile. He called her over. I was going, "No, Brian, don't . . ."

Brian goes, "Hi. Are you Russian?"

She goes, "No. Not Russian," and walks off without elaboration. Perhaps even a little insulted.

I said, "Brian, that's quite a gift you've got there. You want to cultivate that." Brian just laughed and began eyeing the cakes.

We finally moved to the Bush itself for a few rehearsals before previewing. We went into town and bought a costume. Brian wore it all the time. (He even got food on it one night before going on. An elderly man beside me in the audience asked me if the stains were deliberate. I said yes.)

Brian threw a party at his house. We were made to take our shoes off on arrival. At first I was annoyed, thinking this was some bullshit religious observance, until Brian told me to relax, it was just so we'd feel the benefit of his underfloor heating. There was a lot of champagne. A group of us ended up in the back garden, still in our bare feet in what must have been four or five degrees. Those of us not used to champagne invented a character who wants to impress everyone with his rubbish take on the finer things in life.

We left at about seven in the morning.

We opened. Press night had about twenty-five critics. I sat waiting for the moment when Brian says, "Mmm. I was a bollocks to all the other critics. And I'll tell you why, because it was this: they were all cunts." I could remember writing that line one afternoon when I was living with my girlfriend in Leicester. I could remember my mischievous self-satisfaction, thinking what a great fellow I was altogether. And now here it was ringing out over a roomful of critics. There was a silence like someone had pressed the detonator and nothing happened. And then bang, the place erupted. We were all playing.

Brian was fantastic.

I was terrified about how we were going to be received in the papers. Were we having a cheap jibe at an easy target, or were we exploring the nature of reason and responsibility? To tell you the truth I couldn't be sure anymore. If the reviews were bad, I probably wanted the play to be me getting my digs in first. If they were good I wanted the play to induct me and Brian into a community that included artists, audiences *and* critics for however long it lasted. I was a picture of fickle self-preservation.

The morning the reviews came out I was on my way to a reading of my new play, *The Weir*, at the Royal Court. I bought the papers on the way. And I immediately knew we were alright. They knew they'd seen a brilliant piece of acting from Brian, and thankfully that spilled over to include the things he had been able to bring out in my writing. They were bigger men and women than most of us usually give them credit for. But we all suspect that from time to time, in our more self-confident moments perhaps.

I walked into the Royal Court every inch the young-playwright-about-town. More than a bit smug.

Towards the end of the run I went back to the Bush after a sobering few weeks in Dublin. Dominic Dromgoole, who had commissioned *St. Nicholas* before going to work at the Old Vic, came to see the show with his partner Sasha and their new baby Grainne. Grainne was about four weeks old and too young to be left with a sitter. My girlfriend, Rionach, offered to mind her in the dressing room during the show so Sasha could see it and still feed the baby at the interval.

I sat there for a while in the dark dressing room while Rionach walked around with Grainne in her arms. She said, "She keeps moving so she can hear my heart." She slept there, across Rionach's chest. Over the intercom we could hear Brian's performance and I wondered which was putting Grainne to sleep, Rionach's heartbeat or the dead weight of my writing. But I didn't really care. The child in Rionach's arms. And me dripping in lousy perspective.

THE WEIR
JULY 1997

I wrote this play in Leicester where Rionach had a job as an academic. She'd rented a little house, and I sat there avoiding writing. The problem was that I'd worked the play out in my head and writing it down just seemed to damage the idea. I'd write two pages and get up and go for long fraught walks around the suburbs, stopping at the off-license for beer and returning to start preparing dinner for us. Dinner was an endeavor I could drag out for hours. I didn't have to write it.

Finally all these short bursts of writing emerged as a complete narrative, all handwritten. I went back to Dublin and paid my little sister, Margaret, a hundred quid to type it up. I couldn't look at it. I wasn't sure people would think it would work. Some characters telling each other ghost stories in a pub. Were the stories they told any good? Why should we care about the people who told them? I knew I liked them, but why should an audience agree with me? But as my sister typed she kept telling me how much she loved it. She's always been a critical person. She won't watch much television or go to many movies. And she'd never go to a play unless there was a very good reason. She sits reading a book while everyone watches something else. And if she liked *The Weir* it meant it was either very good or completely shite.

I passed the typed script on to Kevin Hely to see what he thought. He rang me the next day to say he hadn't been able to sleep. He'd been scared shitless and kept the light on all night.

I sent it to my agent to pass on to the Royal Court who'd commissioned it. The response was strong. They scheduled it pretty quickly, with Ian Rickson directing. Ian is a man from Lewisham, South London. The play is set in rural Leitrim in the Republic of Ireland. Only six hundred miles away, but worlds apart. We sat in a cramped little patisserie in Soho with Margaret's horrendously typed script in front of us. Ian made notes on it with a pencil. He had few quibbles. I think I agreed to change a few lines and that was it. We were on.

Under no illusions that he knew anything about Ireland, Ian flew over a few weeks later with set designer, Rae Smith. I met them at the airport and we hired a car. The plan was to drive up to Leitrim and do a tour of pubs in the countryside. Rae had her video camera with her. We were looking for ideas. I also wanted to show them the tiny hamlet where I thought the play takes place, Jamestown, with the weir on the Shannon. It had been about two years since I'd been there. And as I showed Ian and Rae around, I had some pangs of guilt and remorse. What gave me the right to situate a piece of fiction so firmly in a real place? I became slightly reluctant to talk about it anymore.

I remembered sitting with my grandad, Jack, in his little house outside Jamestown where he lived alone. Smoking, tipping ash into the fire, drinking bottled stout from a six-pack. And a world, half imagined, half rooted in reality, just about visible to me in the dark. A world of lost afternoons in suburban and rural bars. Of closing your eyes in the dim light, with a community who couldn't or wouldn't judge you.

There was all this stuff in me and it was all very real and I couldn't explain it. We got out of there, and went to bars and places more anonymous to me.

We drove around. Rae sketched things in a book. I showed them Yeats's grave near Ben Bulben. Ian chatted to people in deserted bars, telling them the story of the play. I sat back, a little embarrassed. We ended up in Bundoran where we booked into a hotel. We went to a pub run by two sisters, and Ian told them what we were doing. Some suitable places were suggested to us. This turned into a bit of a session. Ian was our designated driver, and Rae and I were getting steadily pissed.

One bar we went into was tiny. It was Saturday night. The clientele was sitting up at the counter. Middle-aged, chatting away. But as soon as we ordered drinks everything stiffened. Me clearly from Dublin and Ian and Rae (the only woman in the place) with their London accents. The locals threw us curious glances over their shoulders. When we finally left I could sense them relax.

The next morning was beautiful. We went for a walk on the beach after breakfast and then drove back down to Leitrim. This time we went looking for places even more out of the way than the day before. We ended up in the little town of Dromahair. On Sundays in Ireland there's a "holy hour" between two o'clock and four o'clock when you can't buy a drink in a pub. We made it into a cozy bar in Dromahair just before two.

Two men sat at the bar. One at one end and one at the

other. They seemed out of each others' earshot but managed
to have a conversation mainly consisting of grunts and
sighs. The man nearest us was small and skinny. My father
always said that people from Leitrim had a haunted look.
This man had it. High, gaunt cheekbones and an almost
suspicious squinting grin. The other man was round and
wore a shiny suit that had to be twenty years old and worn
every day. His face was red and he wore a cap.

The skinny fellow was drunk in that way that's carried
on from last night. Half hungover, half not knowing what
the hell's wrong with you. He fell into conversation with us.
Where were we from and so on. Ian told him the story of
the play while I drank Guinness, taking the edge off my
own hangover. We in turn got his story of an American
woman who'd moved to Dromahair. This was told with
supportive grunts and indecipherable elaboration from the
round man at the other end of the pub.

She had moved here the previous summer and our skinny
friend, Fergus, had inveigled his way into her life by helping
repair her house, which had been badly built. It turned out
she was married back in America, and though everyone wondered what the hell she was doing, at the same time they just
assumed she was a bit mad. This didn't stop Fergus from
pursuing her, however. And at the bar he slapped his legs
and rubbed his hands together telling us how he'd been the
one to get into bed with her. Yes indeed, him and no one else.
Good God, he'd been riding her morning, noon and night.
Then one day, out of the blue, she decided to go and sort
out her affairs at home in America. But she told Fergus that
her plan was to definitely come back and settle in Dromahair.
She asked him to mind her dogs while she was gone. But
that was a year ago and Fergus was still minding her dogs.
Every day he'd go up to her empty house and feed them,
keeping his foot in the door as it were, waiting for her to
return. Then he rubbed his hands together again in anticipation, and bought ten cans of Budweiser to take with him up
to her house. He liked to get hammered while he fed the dogs.

After our fact-finding mission we returned to Dublin. Rae with her sketchbook and video footage, and me and Ian ready to cast the play. We auditioned people in Dublin and London. The original cast was Brendan Coyle as Brendan, Kieran Ahern as Jim, Julia Ford as Valerie, Jerry Horan as Finbar and Jim Norton as Jack.

The run was only supposed to be for three and a half weeks at the Royal Court in their small sixty-seat venue. We rehearsed in the Drill Hall, off the Tottenham Court Road.

Ian tries to cast ensemble plays with an eye as to how everyone is going to get on with one another. The atmosphere between the actors is important to the quality of their performance together, especially in a play where it's vital that they be seen to be listening to each other. A way that Ian bonds the cast is to bring extra people into the rehearsal room— experts whom the cast can question about what their characters might be experiencing. The first week of rehearsal was spent simply reading the play and talking about it, and then someone would come in and chat to us. We spoke with a bereavement counselor and two experts on the paranormal. The atmosphere was great. We were all learning together and a generosity of spirit seeped into the work.

I went home to Dublin after the first week of rehearsal confident that everything was alright. It was more than that. I found the whole process redemptive and I didn't want to leave. But with drama, for film or for stage, there often comes a point where the person with absolutely nothing more to give is the writer. And no one wants to feel like they're in the way.

I returned for the final week of rehearsal to find everyone in pretty good shape. The set in the Ambassador was extraordinary. The seating was arranged so that the audience was pretty much in the bar with the characters. It had a rare intimacy which must be a joy for any actor to work with.

The dress rehearsals went great, the only problem being me. Nit-picking about blocking and getting on Ian's nerves. And then we started previews. And every night, people in the audience fainted and had to be carried out of the

theatre. It was awful. It usually happened when Julia, as
Valerie, told her story about her daughter. Because these
were previews and nothing had appeared in the papers about
the play, no one knew the story. No one was prepared. And
Julia's performance was devastating. When you've written
something, you forget that each night the audience is hearing it for the first time.

Brain Cox came to the opening night and told me it was
shit. It was the worst play he'd ever seen. I stood gaping at
him, dumbfounded, not only because he seemed to hate it
so much, but also that he'd be so insensitive as to say it to
my face on opening night. But then he couldn't hold back
his laugh. Rionach had got him to wind me up. People with
nothing better to do. I feel sorry for them.

I was staying at Brian's house, and the morning the
reviews came out Ian rang me and told me to buy the papers.
I sleepily went around the corner to a local garage and took
them back to bed with me. And I went back to sleep. I still
feel like the raves we got are a weird dream because of this.

Well, so much for a three-week run. It's early 1999.
There's sun streaming in the windows and *The Weir* is still
running in the West End.

It's strange when people ask me about the success of the
play. I don't feel very responsible. I owe so much to all the
good actors I've learned from. Good actors are out there
doing things by instinct, and so often blessed with excellent
judgment. I'm constantly surprised by them. And often I
receive praise which I know is rightfully theirs.

I've been lucky so far. I've had the opportunity to work
with so many talented people. There's been a lot of laughs,
maybe a bit too much messing, but not too many tantrums.
So here's to lots more late nights and regrettable proclama-
tions. See yous in the bar.

Conor McPherson
Dublin
FEBRUARY 1999

CONOR MCPHERSON was born in Dublin in 1971. He attended University College Dublin where he began to write and direct. He co-founded The Fly by Night Theatre Company in 1992 to produce new plays in Dublin's fringe venues. His work has since been performed internationally, winning numerous awards, including the 1999 Olivier Award for Best Play for *The Weir*, the Stewart Parker award, the George Devine award, a Meyer-Whitworth award, a Critics Circle award, and an *Evening Standard* award. His work for cinema includes *I Went Down*, for which he received a Best Screenplay Award at San Sebastian. Conor McPherson lives in Dublin.